BRIDGE HOUSE SURVIVOR

Experiences of a civilian prisoner-of-war
in Shanghai & Beijing 1942-1945

by

Henry F. Pringle

With an Introduction and Afterword

by

F. Eileen Gray (née Pringle) OAM

Published by Earnshaw Books
Hong Kong 2009

Bridge House Survivor

By Henry F. Pringle

ISBN-13: 978-988-18154-1-5

This book has been reset in 10pt Book Antiqua. Spellings and punctuations are left as in the original edition.

HISTORY / Asia / China

EB020

Published by Earnshaw Books Ltd. (Hong Kong)

CONTENTS

ILLUSTRATIONS

INTRODUCTION

By F. Eileen (Pixie) Gray (née Pringle) OAM

I had no idea in 2008, when I took the decision after a sixty-year absence to visit Shanghai, the city of my birth, that it would lead to the publishing of this book. Sixty years had also passed since my father had completed the typescript for this book and our family had left Shanghai to live in Australia. My father had hoped to publish it in Australia but he died without being able to do so.

My sister, Elizabeth D. Watson and I are deeply grateful to all those who have supported the typescript's publication. We acknowledge particularly Peter Hibbard President of the recently recreated Royal Asiatic Society China in Shanghai and Graham Earnshaw of Earnshaw Books, both of whom are committed to capturing for posterity the past history of China.

Our father, the late Henry (Harry) Forsythe Pringle (1902-1987), wrote this book in the years following the Second World War. It covers the period of his incarceration by Japanese forces in Bridge House and Haiphong Road prisons in Shanghai and in the Fengtai prison near Beijing. He also included a description of his hazardous return trip to Shanghai from Beijing during the chaotic months that followed the end of hostilities in August 1945. In the text he refers to himself as Mr V. I. C. Tim.

Few people were aware of the work's existence. One person who did find it was Greg Leck, who, in his remarkable 2006 publication *Captives of Empire: The Japanese Internment of Allied Civilians in China, 1941-1945*, quoted from a copy which I had placed in the Imperial War Museum in London.

21 Warrane Rd.
Roseville.
N. S. W.
21/8/45

Dear Daddy
            We are aslo happy that you
are no longer a prisoner. We are
having our shcool concert tonight, and
we are all very excited. I hope you will
becoming here soon. I am very ... ...
about you coming tobe with us soon.
I hope that you will be very... ...
when you come. I hope to meet ...
darling daddy soon.

                    Your loving daughter
                        Pixie

        x x x x x x x x x x

Copy of a letter received by the author from one of his daughters after the cessation of hostilities in 1945 – at that time he had not seen his family for four years

Some of my father's own photography has been added to the book. He was the owner of a movie camera — very rare in the 1940s — that the Japanese guards at certain times allowed him to use. Some of these recordings were used as evidence in war crimes trials in later years. Most of the photographs in this book are stills extracted from these motion pictures.

Our family was reunited in Sydney in November 1945 before returning to Shanghai. Our father was in a serious physical and mental condition from which there seemed no recovery. His situation was further complicated when the family was forced, as a result of the communist takeover, to return to Australia. As a result he lost not only his successful career but also his much-loved country of birth.

War extracts an enormous price from all directly and indirectly involved. Our family was no exception and the impact of my father's imprisonment and torture was to continue for many years for all of us. As young children at the time it was difficult for my sister and I to comprehend what was happening. However time is a great healer and understanding has come with age.

Our father never ever recovered completely from his incarceration in Bridge House. As a result of the torture he endured, outbursts of uncontrollable temper frequently occurred during my sister's and my life. How my mother managed to keep her girls quiet during those many episodes of deep emotional torment was a remarkable achievement.

Notwithstanding his rehabilitation over the years, tragically, even in the last few weeks of his life, his experiences under the Japanese Kempeitai were to return to him with all their horror. My father was hospitalised once again during this time. One morning a call was placed by the medical staff on his ward to the school where I was teaching, asking me to please come immediately as my father was in deep distress and was calling for me. As I emerged from the elevator I heard his distraught voice screaming out my name. When I entered the ward I found him with the sides of his bed up, his legs through the bars, shaking them frantically and calling out that the Japanese had imprisoned him again. Earlier that morning he had woken from a deep sleep, found himself in that same situation and had thrown himself over the side onto the floor, opening up his forehead. All I could do at the time, after my initial shock, was to hold and comfort him, assuring him that he was safe, that I was there and that no one could harm him any more. Those memories have never left me.

It would be unforgivable not to pay a special tribute to our late mother Isabella McKendrick Pringle (1894-1983) who in the many dark days carried most of the endless responsibility of healing our father's metaphorical wounds. Scot-tish by birth, she was a highly trained Queen's Nurse, and these special skills were to play an important role in our father's rehabilitation. Her strength and de-termination were to carry us all through what became a frightening time, especially for us young and vulnerable children. The effects of this time remained with us well into our adulthood yet our mother remained steadfast in her faith that she could and would succeed. Her efforts were eventu-ally rewarded after a long and exhausting struggle. She was a saint.

Desmond Pain and John Gray provided invaluable assistance in bringing the publication to fruition. I thank particularly Desmond Pain who digitised the typescript some years ago. I am indebted to Marigold Hogan, Greg Leck, Tom Moore, Eric Niderost, and Desmond Power, for their valuable advice and information. In addition I wish to recognize the encouragement and warm help given by Peter Hibbard, Tess Johnston and Anne Warr, all significant contributors to the documentation of the history of Shanghai.

Finally I express my gratitude to Graham Earnshaw, Andrew Chubb and other staff of Earnshaw Books for the great care with which they have created this book.

F. Eileen Gray
Canberra, Australia

HENRY (HARRY) FORSYTHE PRINGLE

1902-1987

HARRY Pringle was born at Tongshan, China, of British parentage on 20 December 1902. His birth was recorded at the British Consulate-General, Tientsin. His father was a mining engineer who helped the Chinese to establish their coal mines and to build many roads in Shanghai. His mother ran a guest house for the British ex-patriots. Always in the care of Chinese amahs, Harry's first learnt language was Chinese. When his dismayed family realised, they decided Harry and his brother should be speaking English and moved to Shanghai, where the boys attended the American school. Harry went to England after being orphaned at the age of 16, where he joined the Machine Gun Regiment of the Grenadier Guards, in Chatham in December 1919.

He returned to China, arriving in December 1922. He worked in the customs service, the British and American Tobacco Company, and finally the Shanghai Telephone Company, where he remained for over 22 years, rising to Assistant Manager. He belonged to the Shanghai Volunteer Corps and was active in tennis and other sports.

Harry married Isabella McKendrick Holmes at the Cathedral of the Holy Trinity, Shanghai, on 15 April 1932. They raised two children—Elizabeth Doreen and Freda Eileen (a.k.a. Pixie).

Prior to the commencement of the Pacific War, Harry's wife and the two children were evacuated to Australia, arriving there in October 1941. He had intended to follow but before he could do so the war intervened in December 1941. He was imprisoned by Japanese forces as a citizen from 6 October 1942 to 16 August 1945. In November 1945 he travelled to Australia and was reunited with his family.

During 1946 he spent some time in Australia but later returned to Shanghai with his family. He resumed his employment with the Shanghai Telephone Company, and it was during this period that he wrote this manuscript and appeared at two war crime trials. But with the advent of communism in China and the worsening political situation in Shanghai, the family returned to Australia in December 1948.

For the remainder of his life Harry Pringle was a permanent resident of Australia and an Australian citizen. He lived initially at Roseville, a Sydney suburb, and became eventually a Department Manager at Nicholson's Music Store, George Street, Sydney. On his retirement he moved to Canberra, the Australian capital. He was particularly active in several Masonic Orders and achieved high degrees during his many years of membership. He was also very committed to the Liberal Catholic Church and its teachings, and became an ordained Minister.

He visited Shanghai in the 1980s for one day on a Russian cruise ship during which he said a prayer in Jing'an Park for his mother, father and brother, all of whom had been buried there when it was Bubbling Well Cemetery. He also visited Japan a number of times during the post-war years.

Harry Pringle died of heart disease at Canberra on 14 June 1987. His ashes were placed at St. Francis Liberal Catholic Church, Gordon, NSW, beside his dear wife Isabella.

Further information on Harry Pringle's family may be found in the Afterword of this book, an edited transcript of a talk by F. Eileen Gray to the Royal Asiatic Society China in Shanghai on August 29, 2008.

The author before and after the War, 1938 and 1946

BRIDGE HOUSE SURVIVOR

TO THE MEMORY OF THOSE WHO DIED,
BOTH CHINESE AND FOREIGN.
IT IS HOPED THAT THEY DID NOT DIE IN VAIN.

HARRY PRINGLE
SHANGHAI, 1948

AUTHOR'S NOTE

THE story set down in the following pages is a horrible one and it is meant to be so, "Lest We Forget." Every word written is true and the author has in no way drawn on his imagination or exaggerated the facts in the least way. For obvious reasons, the names of the people who suffered have been withheld, with the exception of those who died, and of those Japanese who featured as inquisitors in Bridge House. It may be that many readers of this book will recognize themselves in the descriptions given but every effort has been made to conceal their real identity. It is hoped that this story will impress those people who are inclined to "kiss and make up with the Japs" and that after reading this book, they will realize how careful the leaders of the Allied Nations must be in their dealings with these people, and to make sure that never again will the Japanese nation be placed in the position whereby they can exercise power in any way over their fellow men.

There are, no doubt, many Japanese who are cultured and gentle people. The author came in contact with a few of these and owes to them a debt of thanks which he believes has since been repaid but unfortunately the good ones were by far in the minority and their good deeds, for their own sakes, had to be done under the cover of secrecy. Unfortunately, many of the guilty ones have escaped justice, and it is feared that the day is too late in hoping that they will eventually be brought to justice. It is too much to hope that people of that type and character will ever suffer through their consciences. They are beyond that.

V.I.C. T

Shanghai, October 6th, 1948

CHAPTER I
SHANGHAI, 1942

THE Pacific war had been going on for ten months and we, in Shanghai, had not felt the horrors to the extent that the peoples of other lands and cities had felt them. It is true that we were all living under the shadow of the Rising Sun and all that it meant, but we still did not realize what war really meant. On the advice of our representative Consular bodies, we had continued our work as usual in the various utility companies under Japanese domination. We had been assured by our conquerors that provided we did not indulge in any subversive activity that we had nothing to fear but knowing the Japanese as I did, I did not put much faith in their assurances.

Personally, I had predicted that as soon as our usefulness to them had come to an end they would get tough with us. Many of my friends pooh-poohed this idea, saying that the Japanese needed us and that as Shanghai itself was a vast concentration camp, we did not have much to fear. These optimists pointed to those who had already been thrown out of employment, saying that they had not been interned and therefore what had we to fear? My reply to this was that had they commenced to intern those who were not employed, this would have brought about a lowering of the standard of work the Japanese were getting out of us who were employed, and would also encourage wholesale attempts at escaping from the Shanghai area. This would, of course, have necessitated the deviation of thousands of men from the active fronts for the purpose of guarding the boundaries of Shanghai to prevent such escapes. My predictions were only too true.

Immediately after Pearl Harbour, a few leading British and American business men and journalists, amongst whom was the late journalist and China hand J. B. Powell, were immediately arrested and taken to the infamous Gendarmerie Headquarters known as "Bridge House." We heard rumours that they had been badly tortured and were being detained under the most unspeakable conditions of filth and misery, but as nobody could see them, this could not be verified. Those who were fortunate to eventually be released were too frightened to talk, but from one of these I had obtained certain information which bore out the truth of what we had heard was going on in Bridge House. His story filled me with horror, and whilst I was not doing anything which might have been termed subversive, I realized that any of us might fall under suspicion. During the summer of 1942, I had been more or less actively engaged in assisting the local Soviet Community in raising funds for their Red Cross, my argument being that this could not be considered as subversive and as I could not in any way serve my own country, that the least I could do was something for the wounded of our Ally. As the months wore on, I thought that I was getting away with this and then came that day which will forever live in my memory as the blackest day of my life—October 6th, 1942.

CHAPTER II
BRIDGE HOUSE PRISON

OCTOBER 6th 1942 was one of those beautiful Shanghai autumn days, still quite warm with the sun shining brightly and making one feel good to be alive. The morning at the Office was humdrum and monotonous as it had been from the start of the war. I went home to tiffin at noon and had one of my favourite feeds, namely, mince beef, rice and vegetables. It is funny how one remembers little things like that. I had arranged with a very dear friend that I would meet her at one of the local clubs at half past seven that evening, and after having made this arrangement and looking forward to the evening, I returned to the Office.

At about twenty minutes past two, my telephone bell rang and the following conversation took place, "Hello, this is Koshino."

"Good afternoon, Mr. Koshino. What can I do for you?"

"Are you in your Office?" he asked.

"Of course, I am. What do you want?" I replied.

"Oh, nothing. I just wanted to see. Thank you."

I put down the receiver mildly wondering what it was all about. I did not have to wait long, as a few minutes afterwards the door opened and in walked Shinohara, the Japanese General Manager of the Company, followed by eight of the toughest Japs I have seen.

I rose to my feet as my first thought was that this was one of the usual parties of Japs being shown around the building, which at that time the Japanese were doing a lot of. They were quite proud of their acquisition. However, Shinohara walked up to me and said, "Are you Tim?"

"Yes, I am." I replied.

Then he introduced his party, "These gentlemen are from the Japanese Gendarmerie and they want you to go with them to their Headquarters, as they have a few questions to ask you."

"Is there anything wrong, Mr. Shinohara?"

"I don't know" he replied.

In the meantime, the "gentlemen" had gathered around my desk in a semi-circle with their hands in their jacket pockets. It was quite apparent that they had guns.

I picked up my jacket and three of them escorted me out of the building and politely asked me to please step in their car. Needless to say, I was horribly frightened but wishing to test out just how serious the matter was, I asked if I might smoke. My escort very politely gave me permission to do so, even offering me a light. This made me feel better and so we proceeded to Bridge House, but at the entrance to the Office, their demeanour changed as one of them barked, "Put out cigarette! Go inside!"

I went in and leant against one of the chairs with my hand in my pocket and waited. Suddenly, a voice barked across the Office, "Take your hand out of your pocket or else I shall slap your face, you English bastard."

Needless to say, I had never pulled my hand out of my pocket so quickly in my life before. Then one of them came up to me and ordered me to sit down and proceeded to question me as to my name, age, nationality and so forth, entering all these details on a form, after which he ordered me to empty my pockets and remove my necktie and belt. All articles so removed were duly entered on the form and I was asked to remember "all things."

The "gentleman" who had barked at me, came over and putting his hands on his hips said, "This is Bridge House and you are going inside and if you speak inside I will cut your damn head off. You understand?"

I replied that I did. I was then taken out through the back door and then into another back door. My escort tightly clutching my arm, knocked on a door. I heard bolts being shot back and the door was opened by a Gendarme in uniform. I was roughly pushed in and got my first sight of the cages. The stench that struck my nostrils was terrible, and the sight that met my horrified eyes was something that I shall never forget. I saw three bearded miserable faces peering at me through the bars of the cage. One of them was that of a friend, but I did not recognize him. I did not have much time to see more because I was roughly pulled around and the guard on duty began to take down details of my name, etc. He barked out "Sango" which meant third cell. I was then hustled along the passage and was halted before a wooden barred door, where I was ordered to take my shoes off, which were placed in a sort of cupboard where there were many other pairs of shoes. The doors of the cell were opened and I was pushed in.

This cell was in reality a cage with solid wooden walls on two sides and bars also of wood on the other two sides. It measured 19' x 11' and into this space were crammed twenty human beings, men and women. When I arrived, there were three other white people, two men and one woman and sixteen Chinese, all men. They were sitting in rows on the floor which consisted of a sort of platform raised about 2' above the concrete floor. In one corner, in a sort of alcove, was the lavatory bucket whence came the terrible stench. I eventually discovered that there were ten such cages in this section of the gaol with similar conditions existing in all of them. The cages were situated in what had been garages, which were part of the Bridge House apartments.

A space on the edge of the platform was pointed out to me by one of my fellow prisoners and I sat down. I was too terror stricken to even think and could only sit there staring in front of me. Eventually my nerves calmed down a bit and I looked around. Three of my fellow prisoners were smothered in a loathsome skin disease. All were in varying stages of emaciation. One

BRIDGE HOUSE PRISON

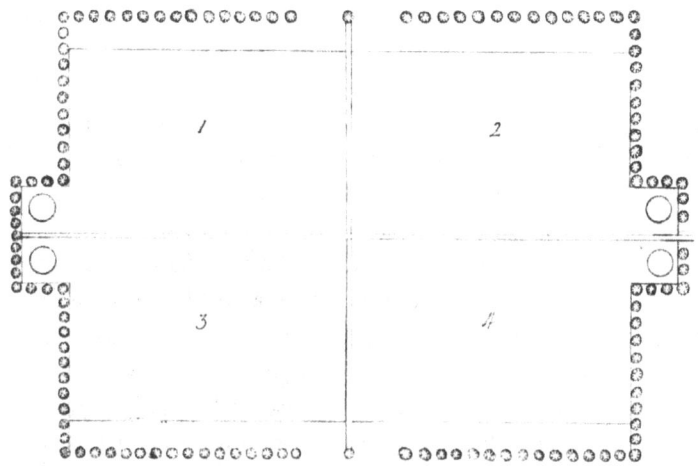

GROUND PLAN OF CELL BLOCK

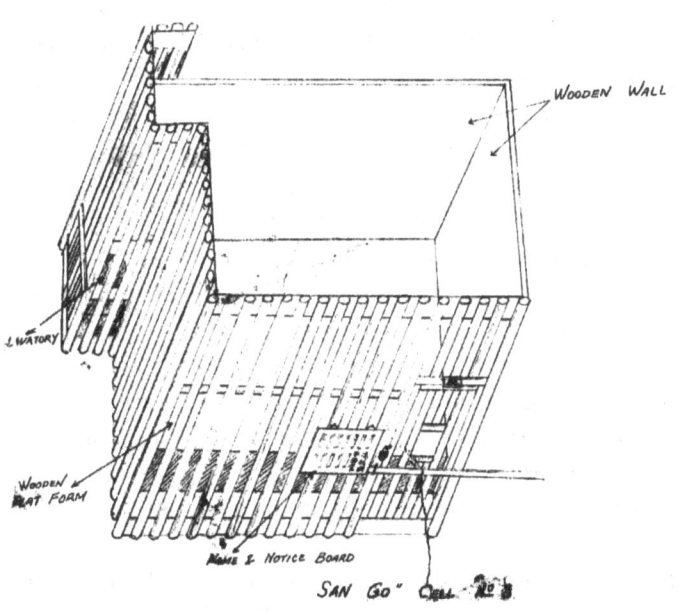

Plan of Bridge House prison cells by Henry Pringle

of the other foreigners came near me and asked me in a whisper who I was and what my case was. I told him my name but told him also, that why I had been brought here I did not know. We entered into a whispered conversation and he informed me that he had been there since 6th August and that as far as he could make out, they had not nearly finished with his case. The story that he told of his sufferings was horrible in the extreme.

Ali (for that was his name) told me that his fiancee had been arrested the day before he had. His own arrest had been almost accidental as he had telephoned to her and an obviously Japanese voice had answered his call. Being exceedingly worried, he had walked around to his fiancee's house and was about to turn in at the apartment house entrance, when a party of Japanese plain clothes men were just on the point of leaving. He turned away, but was called back by one of the Japs who asked him who he was. He told them, giving them his name. They asked him what his nationality was and he said he was an Iranian. They told him he could go and he had only taken about a dozen paces when he heard one of them say, "Oh Iranian. Enemy subject. Hey! Come back." He went back to them and was told that he was under arrest. He was removed to Bridge House and was immediately questioned. His questioning occupying something like twelve hours without a stop. He denied knowing anybody living in that particular apartment and when they accused him of being a member of a big Russian spy ring, he had laughed at them and denied it.

They put him into the cell that night and the next day had resumed questioning him. Finding threats of violence of no avail, one of them asked him if he was thirsty. As the liquid ration was very low, consisting of only half a glass of tea per day and the weather being extremely hot, he naturally said, "Yes, very thirsty."

They all laughed uproariously at his reply and told him that they would give him a good drink. A kettle of water was brought into the room and he put his hand out for it, but they said, "No, no, we will help you." They ordered him to lie on the floor and when he refused, he was promptly knocked down and tied to rings on the floor. A wet towel was slapped over his face and he got his drink! Kettle after kettle being poured into his nose and mouth. Finding this ineffectual, they had beaten him with dog whips. They found this of no use, so simply yelling with rage, they beat and kicked him around the room. He was then carried half conscious back to the cell and thrown into it.

They left him alone for a couple of days and then had taken him up again and suddenly opening the door, had thrust him into another room where he saw his fiancee seated in a chair, obviously terrified and in pain. She started to her feet and cried out his name. Of course, that gave the game away and finding it useless to deny his acquaintance with her any longer, he admitted that he knew her. They took him out and asked him if he had negotiated a draft for US$ for her. Having done this, he admitted it, but said that beyond knowing her very well and having done this favour for her, he knew nothing else.

Then commenced a period of absolute horror for him. He told them repeatedly that no matter what they did, he would not admit to having done something which he had not done. They beat him, burnt him, strung him up by his thumbs, tied ropes to his ankles whilst he was in a sitting position and bent his knees in the wrong direction, they placed angle iron bars across his shin bones on which two men sat for half an hour till he was nearly insane with the pain, they tied him to the wall and turned a savage dog loose on him and finally took him down to the swimming bath and nearly drowned him. Ali was indeed a superman. He never gave way and never admitted anything. At a later date, I saw a Japanese guard stick a bayonet point into his knee, and he never uttered a sound beyond looking the Japanese in the eye and saying to him, "You dirty Japanese bastard." For once I saw a Japanese appear to be absolutely ashamed, of himself.

After hearing of these horrors, you can well imagine what my own feelings were. Ali said to me, "You do not have to worry too much about that, as your case might mean nothing and you will soon be able to obtain your release. Just put on a bold front and you will be all right."

I asked him how long it would be before I would be taken up for questioning and he replied that it all depended on whether the Japs had anything definite on me and which, if they had, they would have me up right away or whether they had to do a lot of investigating before taking any action.

By this time, it was nearly five o'clock. Through the bars we saw another victim being brought along. He was thrown into our cell and turned out to be a sixty-two year old Englishman named Douglas Fleming. The Japanese pronounced his name "Fleshing." He had been brought in on a framed-up charge. They alleged that he knew something about two other Britons who had been arrested on the grounds of being in the pay of the British Government. Old Pop, as we called him, had strenuously denied this.

By that time, I had begun to settle down a little bit and looked around and tried to get acquainted with my fellow unfortunates. One of them was a dear old chap of sixty-three years of age, a Russian Jew named Podolsky. He had already been in twenty-five days and, for his age, was bearing up remarkably well. He had not, as yet, been questioned in any way. Another inmate was a respectable Russian woman whom I shall call Shura, aged forty-six. She had been in since September 8th and I have never seen anybody so utterly terror-stricken as she was. A Jap had only to look at her and she would commence to tremble like an aspen leaf. Incidentally, her place in the cell was right beside the lavatory bucket. I will never forget my embarrassment when nature made its demands and I had to use the bucket for the first time in front of her. I remember very timidly and embarrassedly asking her pardon. She looked at me with great surprise. However, one soon got over one's embarrassment in this respect. The remaining prisoners in the cell consisted of sixteen Chinese, all males.

At half past five, we received our dinner which consisted for the foreigners or white people of 4 oz. of dry bread and a little sip of tea. The Chinese received a bowl of boiled rice and also a sip of tea. At seven o'clock, we heard shouts of "Tenko, Tenko" from the Japanese guards. We all jumped up and lined up in two ranks. The cell captain stood at the right and when the door of the cell was thrown open and in strode two Japs, he shouted, "Tehyotsikeh" which is the equivalent of "Attention." He then shouted "Kerrei" and we all had to bow. The cell captain then gave a report of the number of prisoners present and of those who were being questioned and of those who were too weak to stand up and were lying in what we called the "Dying Corner." The Jap and his escort then inspected the prisoners and I remember his finding one Chinese who did not have his heels together and he kicked his ankles which brought the unfortunate wretch to the floor in pain. Both Japs roared with laughter. As they were leaving the cell, the cell captain called out "Kerrei." The Jap standing rigidly to attention replied with a dignified salute.

This procedure, I was informed, was observed morning and evening and sometimes during the day and night. When the "Tenko" or "Roll Call" was over, we were permitted to take our exercise which consisted of getting in a circle and pounding around and around like so many caged rats. As we were tramping on a platform, the drumming of feet on the floor sounded like war drums. I will never forget that sound. After this we returned to our positions and just sat and gazed at nothing.

At nine o'clock, the guards came around and called out, "Moppu," which I was told meant, "Come and get your blankets." Two bundles of blankets were carried into the cell and mine turned out to be a very worn out filthy cotton blanket. We then composed ourselves on the floor, and attempted to sleep. I remember dropping off into a fitful slumber, but awakened with a start when I heard screams coming from some part of the building above us. These screams continued most of the night and were from some unfortunate wretches being "treated." When morning finally did come, we were awakened by a shout, "Sho" and then were told in Chinese to hurry up. I never did discover why we had to hurry.

The foreigners were permitted to go into the back yard to perform their ablutions, which was done under a tap. I will never forget how sweet the outside air smelt after the fug and stench indoors, but we were not given much time and within three or four minutes, were herded back to our cells where we sat again until eight o'clock, when we got our breakfast which consisted of a bowl of congee. Congee is nothing else than well boiled rice and water, and plenty of the latter, in which the rice was boiled. During the day, nothing happened to relieve the terrible monotony. Little did I know that one hundred and fourteen such days lay before me. Lunch finally dragged around and for lunch, the foreigners received 4 oz. of dry bread, the Chinese, boiled rice. None of my captors came near me and day followed day until I was wondering if they had forgotten my existence.

Poor old Pop Fleming was taken out of the cell at about nine o'clock in the morning after his arrest. He returned at eleven thirty in a terrible state. They had beaten him with rods, given him the salt water treatment and had strung him up by his thumbs. In addition to that, they had amused themselves by shaving off his eyebrows and clipping off his eyelashes. The poor old fellow was absolutely speechless. I went to his assistance as soon as he came into the cell but the Chinese warned me not to help him as I would get into trouble myself. I told them to go to hell, and did my best to make the poor old fellow comfortable. Ali, the Iranian, also assisted me, as he did not care a damn for any Jap that ever walked.

Then came the night of October 13th-14th, 1942.

CHAPTER III
THE TORTURERS

B Y this date I had, more or less got used to my surround-
ings, to the lice, bed bugs, mosquitoes, flies, rats and had
also learned to sleep soundly on a hard floor, wrapped
only in a blanket. My horror had been increased because I found
that they had arrested my very good friend T, and had put her in
a cell, adjacent to mine. She, poor thing, was just as ignorant as
myself as to the cause of our arrest. On the morning of October
13th, just as I was coming in from having had my wash, one of
the guards had jokingly slapped my back and challenged me to
a pushing competition. He invited me to push him as hard as I
could. I said, "Nothing doing. If I push you too hard, you will
beat me up."

He roared with. laughter at this and assured me that he would
not. He then gave me a push which sent me half way along
the corridor and taking him at his word, I let go at him and he
crashed up against the wall. It shook him up a bit, but he took it
in very good part. He then challenged me to a race up and down
the corridor. Being bare footed, I left him standing and was back
again before he got to the end. This amused him vastly and he
told me that I was a "berry" good fellow. He opened the door
of the cell and playfully kicked me on the behind and laughed
uproariously when I tripped and rolled across the floor. He was
a brute at heart but no doubt thought himself a fine chap. I remember later on he came into our cell one day with the padlock
of the cell in his hand and told all the prisoners to hurry and

get to the other end of the cell. I evidently did not move quickly enough and he swung the padlock at me and caught me across the hand. It severed a small artery and I bled like a stuck pig. He was very amused about this but later he handed me in a bandage and some ointment.

I went to "bed" at the usual time on the night of Tuesday, October 15th, and had. been asleep a couple of hours when I felt something jabbing me in the back and woke up and saw a Japanese in civilian clothes standing outside the cell, poking me with a long piece of bamboo and telling me to get up and come. I realized that this was "IT." They had not taken my glasses from me when I was put inside and I took the precaution of leaving these behind when I left the cell. They took me into the same Office that I had come into at the time of my arrest and then up some stairs where there was a sort of mezzanine floor. There were cubicles all along one side and I was taken into one of these. Seated therein were seven men, all very brutal in appearance.

One of them in good English said, "Good evening Mr. Tim. Come inside and sit down. Would you like a cigarette?" and needless to say, I took one.

They offered me coffee and sandwiches, all of which I very gratefully accepted as I was very hungry despite my fear. Then the English speaking one said, "Mr. Tim, we have a few questions to ask you which we hope you will be perfectly frank in answering. We do not want to have any trouble with you and if you answer frankly, you will soon be released from this not very pleasant place, but if you are not frank with us, I am afraid that you will suffer."

I replied that as I had nothing to conceal, I was quite prepared to be perfectly frank and honest with them. They all smiled and said this was very good and that they were glad.

They produced a few scraps of paper which had been found in my desk and asked me the meaning of what was written thereon. I evidently answered to their satisfaction, as they threw the papers aside. Then they produced a map which I had had in my desk in the Office and asked me why I had the map there. I explained to them that back in 1934 right up to 1940, I had been very fond of walking in the country and had used this map during my walks. They noticed that I had put some red and blue ink marks on the map and asked me the meaning of this. My explanation to this was that they represented the Shanghai-Hangchow motor highway and that I had put those marks on when the highway was first built as I often used to motor to Hangchow. This answer also appeared to satisfy them.

The next thing they produced was a file in which there were a number of statements of accounts for the Japanese Gendarmerie, Naval and Army authorities. These were dated 1938 and represented unpaid accounts for a certain period after the conclusion of the Sino-Japanese hostilities in the Shanghai area. I explained this to them very carefully when one of them banged the desk and yelled out, "Lie!" He shouted out something in Japanese and the interpreter told me that the gentleman said that I had kept this file in my desk for the purpose of keeping a record of all official Japanese lines and that I had used this for the purpose of listening in to secret conversations. I laughed at this, as it really was ridiculous and told them quite truthfully that I only knew about ten words of Japanese and therefore how could I have listened to their conversation. The man who had shouted first then thundered out something else in Japanese at considerable length. The interpreter said that it was well known that a strong spy organization had been set up within the Telephone Company. He proceeded to reel off names saying that so and so was the Head, so and so was the Technical Man, so and so was the Russian Liaison, so and so (Koreans) were listeners in, so and so was the Chinese who obtained information from outside and that I was the second in command who arranged for all information to be passed to the Soviet authorities.

Needless to say, I was dumb-founded at these misstatements. The whole thing was a tissue of lies and I told them so. The interpreter who informed me that his name was Jimmy then said that Mr. Jackie (pointing to the man in charge of the investigation) said that as I had asked for trouble and would not be frank, they would have to take it out of my body. To say that I was not frightened would be absolutely untrue. Frankly, I was absolutely terror-stricken and vividly recalled the shrieks of agony which I heard every night. I kept saying over and over again to them, "You are absolutely mistaken. I know nothing about these accusations and ask you to produce the person who has laid this false information against me." They ignored me completely.

All of them rose and walked out of the room with the exception of Jimmy. He, speaking very quietly told me that I could avoid all trouble by readily admitting my guilt, and that the worst that would happen to me was that of being sentenced to a few years in gaol. I replied that I could not admit to anything that was so patently false and that to do so would involve other also innocent people. For twenty minutes he tried to persuade me to confess, but I continued to deny everything. He then shrugged his shoulders and said that he could do no more to help me, and that I had to take the consequence. He told me to follow him downstairs.

When I got downstairs in the Office, I saw that they had prepared two benches side by side and were getting out ropes and various other pinioning paraphernalia. One man was testing out an electric shocking device. I was ordered to sit down at a desk and when I had done so, they placed a piece of paper and a pencil in front of me and told me that I had ten minutes to write a farewell letter to my wife, as I was going to die. My reply was, "If you murder me tonight, it is your responsibility and not mine to notify my wife."

One of them struck me savagely across the face for this, but they left the paper and pencil in front of me and started in counting off the minutes. "Nine minutes — eight — seven — six — five — four — three — two — one. It is too late. You have had your chance. Now get ready to die."

They told me to lie down on the benches but before doing so,

I knelt for a moment and commended my spirit and prayed for strength. They stood by in utter silence, while I was doing this. I laid down on the bench and they proceeded to strap me down, then pulled down my trousers and bared my whole body. Then they asked me if I would speak and I replied that I had nothing to say. One of them clapped a towel over my eyes and held my head down, whilst another sprayed water over my body. Once more, they asked me to speak and I shook my head. The next thing I remember was a searing shock passing through my body as they applied an electrode to my navel and then commenced passing the other electrode over my breast, lips, throat, eyes and ears.

The agony was terrible and I shrieked with pain. My convulsions caused the benches to overturn and I was writhing on the floor still tangled up with the ropes. They quickly untied me and set up the benches again and ordered me to lie down a second time. I refused to do so and with that, five of them sprang at me and knocked me over and then lifted my body on to the benches, this time putting handcuffs around my ankles and using another two pairs, clamped these ankle cuffs down to the legs of the benches. I was then roped down so that I could not move a muscle. After these operations, they continued with the electrical torture.

They laid the electrodes on the tenderest parts of my body and I thought that I was going mad. I repeatedly tried to bash my head against the bench, but I could not knock myself out. Fortunately, I passed out, but was revived with hot coffee. They came at me again with the electrodes, but this time I had taken a firm grip of myself and was able to take it without screaming. They stopped with the electricity, but I was unable to see what they were up to next. I heard water being poured out and it flashed through my mind that I was going to get the water treatment. Suddenly, I felt one of them sit down on my stomach, and a wet towel was placed across my mouth and nose and then I felt the water being poured on it. I thrashed about, trying to dodge the stream of water but then feeling my lungs almost bursting, I began to gulp. I did not know how much water they poured into me. Every now and then, the swine who was sitting on my stomach, jumped up and down. This forced all the water up into my mouth, but being unable to expel it, I had to swallow my own vomit. Again I passed out. When I came to, the interpreter Jimmy began to shriek, "Speak, you bastard, speak!" and I gasped out, "I have nothing to say."

I felt a terrible burning sensation on one of my feet and later discovered that they had burnt my foot with cigarette butts. Then they continued the water treatment and alternated it with the electrical treatment. This went on for a total of six awful, horrible hours.

I do not remember being released, but was told later that I was brought back into the cell at half past eight in the morning. They had started their torture at two in the morning! I was thrown into the cell and as soon as the guards were gone, dear old Ali, dragged my unconscious body into a corner, and wrapped me in a blanket. For two days, I was not aware of much that was going around me. One thing I remember clearly and that was having hallucinations. I imagined that I saw my wife, my brother and my mother looking at me through the windows and shaking their heads in sorrow. It was so vivid that I asked Ali why they were watching me. He recognized the first signs of insanity and lifting me to my feet, he slapped me across the face and said, "Don't give in, you bastard, pull yourself together." He then proceeded to walk me around and around the cell.

Night-time was horrible. The silence punctuated at times by screams made the night endless. After forty-eight hours, I began to become more myself. I found that my wrists had been gashed open by the ropes, and my left wrist was already festering. A lump had formed under my arm and I had visions of blood poisoning. A Japanese nurse passing by the cell on her way to look at a dying prisoner in another cell saw my wrists and pitied my horrible condition. She expressed concern and told me that she would return later with some medicines. She was as good as her word and her ministrations no doubt saved my arm, if not, my life. Several times during the course of the next few days, my inquisitors came to look at me and asked me how my body was. Ali had warned me never to say that you are feeling all right, always say, "I am very sick." You might get away with something that way. They left me alone for ten days, but during this period another tragedy was being enacted, Poor old Podolsky was dying.

CHAPTER IV
THE DEATH OF PODOLSKY

PODOLSKY'S arrest had been effected twenty-five days before my own, and I was surprised to see how well the old chap had stood up to his incarceration. He had been receiving the same diet as the rest of us had, which made his condition all the more surprising. He had not been questioned up to the time of my arrival and was beginning to have hopes of early release. In this he was due for disappointment as on the thirty-seventh day after his arrest, he was taken up for questioning. After three hours, he was brought back to the cell in a state of utter collapse. I asked him if they had beaten him up at all and he said "No," but that unless he answered their questions to their satisfaction, they were going to give him the "works" the next time.

I endeavoured to cheer him up by saying that as they had not struck him on the occasion of the first questioning, that they were just bluffing and that he should not worry.

About an hour after his return to the cell, he toppled over in a dead faint. We brought him around again, as there was a decent guard on duty who gave us some water with which we washed him down and refreshed him a little bit. The poor old fellow hardly slept a wink that night, as they had told him that they were coming for him again the next day. As I suspected, they were bluffing, because he was not called up again, until the forty-second day.

He was away for about two and a half hours, and again returned, trembling with fear and terror. He said that they had not beaten him up, but had shouted and stormed at him for two hours and that they had threatened that the next time they called him, he would be given the water treatment. This was too much for him and he began to visibly fade away. When I came to the cell on October 6th, he was still quite stout, but after his two questionings, he had lost at least thirty to thirty-five pounds in weight. I have never seen a man collapse so quickly. On the forty-seventh day, he was in such a weakened state that we had to carry him to the lavatory. He was beginning to lose control of his bowels which made our task terribly unpleasant.

We told our friendly guard that we thought he was dying and that he had better notify the higher ups. He evidently did so, because late in the evening three of them came to see him. They appeared rather concerned about his condition and promised that they would call up his wife and get her to send some food to him, besides a change of clothing. For once they kept their promise, because the next day a basket containing some real food was delivered. We in the cell, immediately got to work and tried to feed the old man with some of the nourishing chicken broth which had been sent in, but by this time it was too late and he could not keep it down. On the evening of the fifty-second day, it was obvious to all that the old chap was finished.

At about six o'clock, I called the attention of the guard to the fact that the old man was dying. I used the Chinese expression, "Chobitsu," which literally translated means, "he is going to eat his own queue." The guard was of a particularly brutal type and yelled out at me, "Nie chobitsu," which meant, "Not dying." He ordered me to leave Podolsky alone, which order I ignored, and again went to the old chap to see if I could do anything for him. This infuriated the guard and he ordered me to come back to the bars and kneel down on the concrete floor. To have refused to have done so would have meant being half killed so I knelt and he reached through the bars with a thin iron pipe and struck me on the head and on both shoulders. The blows nearly paralysed both my arms.

After recovering Ali and I again did our best to get Podolsky to swallow some nourishment. This he could not do, as he had sunk into a sort of coma. Shortly after this, a Japanese prisoner who was a sort of trusty, came to the bars of the cell and, beckoning to me, whispered that he knew that Podolsky was to be released the next day and sent home. I got Shura to repeat over and over to him in Russian, that he was going home tomorrow. It seemed to penetrate and for a little while revived him! The rally however, did not last, because at ten minutes past nine, Podolsky died. Another victim of Japanese terrorism.

I again called the attention of the guard who had beaten me and told him that Podolsky had died. He would not believe me, so I turned Podolsky's face towards him. He gave one look, shouted something and rushed off. Five minutes later, several of the Japanese who were in charge accompanied by a nurse carrying a hypodermic syringe, rushed into the cell. The nurse immediately went over to Podolsky, bared his breast, but after feeling him, looked up and shook her head. One of the Japanese who could speak excellent English named Watanabe, turned around and shouted at me, "Why did you not tell the guard that he was so sick?" For an answer, I showed him the lump on my forehead and the two bruises on my shoulders and said, "I did, and this is what I got for my trouble."

The senior man present, whose name I later learned was Yokohata, turned around on the guard and started shouting at him at the top of his voice. The guard stood at attention saying nothing, but rapidly bowing. He left under the escort of another guard and we never saw him again. It occurred to me at that time, that they did not like having white men die in the cells. Watanabe turned to me and said very politely, "Please you and three others carry him out."

We lifted him up and carried him out into the backyard, and covered him with some corrugated iron, after which Ali and I standing side by side, bowed in reverence to him. The Japs snapped their heels together and also bowed. The four of us were about to return to the cell but were called back and were each given a cigarette. We asked if we might wash ourselves and Watanabe replied, "Anything, anything."

I learned after the war, that Mrs. Podolsky had been informed the next day of her husband's death and had been ordered to take over his body. At the Jewish Cemetery, when she saw him, she refused to believe that the pitifully shrunken form lying before her was the body of her husband.

CHAPTER V
VONG AND POP FLEMING
GO DOWN

TWO days after Podolsky's death, I was again taken up for questioning into the same cubicle that I had been taken to on the first occasion. The same eight men were present. These are the names of five of them: Yokohata, Watanabe, Suzuki, Nakatani and the interpreter "Jimmy" Yokomizo. They were standing in a circle and all were holding kendo sticks, which are the sticks they use when practising sword play and are made of split bamboo, bound at intervals with twine. I was thrust into the middle of the circle and Jimmy said, "You had better speak." I asked them what they wanted to know. The reply was, "You know. Speak!"

I said, "How can I speak, if I don't know what you want." Jimmy who had spent the last eighteen years in the United States and had a fine command of American slang yelled out, "You know god damn well what we want to know, so you better speak and save yourself a beating up."

I replied again that I did not know what they wanted. The next thing I knew was getting a stunning blow on the back of the head with a kendo stick and at the same time a push. This sent me to the other side of the circle and I was promptly knocked back again. How many times they punched me around that circle, I do not know, because I went down on the floor under a shower of blows. They did not let me lie for long, but started on me with their boots and got me to my feet again. How long this went on for I have no idea, as I mercifully passed out. When I came to, they had all left with the exception of Jimmy and Yokohata. I was sitting in a chair and Jimmy was throwing water into my face.

When I had collected my wits sufficiently, he offered me a cigarette and a drink of water and said, "You know you lug, if you would only speak and tell us the truth, you would save yourself a lot of trouble." I replied, "How can I speak, when I have nothing to say, have done nothing and know nothing?"

"Well, you are only a god damn fool and you have only yourself to blame for all your trouble."

I replied, "What is the use of my saying anything, if what I say is a lot of bunk and after investigation by you, proves to be just that. You will only take it out of me for giving you a wild goose chase."

"Oh, come off that line." he said. "You know we have arrested A, B, C and the two X sisters as well as S and also your Russian pal P. They have already confessed and so you might as well."

Knowing this to be an old gag, I asked that they be brought before me and confirm that statement. My reward for this bright remark was a good sound slap across my face. Yokohata then came into the picture and spoke at length to Jimmy. Jimmy then turned around to me and said, "There is a repatriation ship going soon and if you spill the beans, we guarantee you will go on that ship." I replied that I would be very glad to go on the ship and that if it was in my power to accept the offer, I would have considered it, but my position and reply to this offer was just as it was the first night, I had nothing to say. Then he said, "You know the water is getting damned cold now and another dose of that would just about freeze your guts. Do you want another dose?" I naturally replied "No."

"Well, we will let you go back now," said Jimmy, "and we will have you up tomorrow and if you have not got the answers ready, Christ help you." I was then returned to the cell full of foreboding and really scared out of my wits.

I could hardly sleep at all that night and about two o'clock in the morning, was awakened from a troubled sleep by yells of pain. I then witnessed another example of Jap brutality. They had dragged in a bare footed Chinese dressed in black, obviously of the beggar type. They were giving him a hell of a beating and his shrieks for mercy were echoing through the whole building. They kept on pouring buckets of icy water on him and then warming him up with sticks. This went on for the best part of an hour and a half. I saw them put a pair of handcuffs on him and he was then brought to our cell and thrown into it. He was made to stand on the cold concrete for the rest of the night.

The next morning when the breakfast of congee was served out, we noticed that there were only eleven bowls given to our cell. Our numbers were now twelve including the new comer. We asked the trusty about this and he told us that written on the cell notice boards outside the door was an order: "No food, no drink for Vong." At the same time, the guard showed up and made Vong, which was the new comer's name, stand with his back to the bars and watch us eat. He told him in Chinese, "We are going to starve you to death. We'll teach you to steal from us." After he had left, we found out that Vong was a petty thief who had had the audacity to come over the Gendarmerie compound wall with a pal and steal three small bars of iron. He got away with it the first time and an hour later returned for some more. This time he had been spotted and caught.

At first we did not believe that the Japanese really meant to starve him, but what followed showed us how little we knew the gentle Jap. For the first week after his arrest, we passed bits of our own food to Vong. At the end of a week, they came in to look at him and were much surprised to see him looking so well. They turned around to us and said that they knew we were feeding him and that if they saw one bite of food being handed to him, they would stop the whole cell's food for a week. Well, self preservation is the first law of nature and we told Vong just that. He shrugged his shoulders and said, "Mei yu fah dze shang," in other words, "it is so fated, so there is no use in complaining," and then proceeded to calmly accept his fate. I had never seen such heroism and cheerfulness in a man who was bred in the gutters of Shanghai and was a member of China's lowest class. In the days that followed, the Japanese guards would come in almost every day and subject his poor body to terrible beatings. I have seen a guard get him into a corner and hold him down with his booted foot, while he beat him over his head with a piece of wood, until the unfortunate wretch was shrieking for mercy, and then would just haul off and kick him in the stomach and laughingly leave the cell. On one occasion, as he was beginning to get so thin, he managed to slip the handcuff off his wrist, one of the guards caught him and beat his hands with a rope end until they were a bloody pulp. After this, he forced the handcuffs over his hands, tearing the torn flesh on his hands still more.

He first of all became terribly emaciated and his head looked like a skull. About the twenty-fifth day, the left side of his face blew up to a terrific size and then the right side did the same. By the night of the twenty-fifth day, he was completely blind and was crawling around the floor. Parched with thirst, he was drinking his own urine. On the evening of the twenty-sixth day, they came in to look at him once more and said, "Good, this will teach you. Tomorrow you can feed him."

I had kept a little bit of bread hidden and on the guards leaving the cell, I had pulled the bread from its hiding place, which was between my legs and making up little pellets, attempted to feed him. Our decent guard was on duty again and gave me a cup of water which I let him drink in very tiny sips. He moaned all that night. The next morning, a bowl of congee was passed in for him and we attempted to feed this slowly to him, but the poor fellow was too far gone and could not swallow it. By ten o'clock, he lapsed into a coma and died at three o'clock in the afternoon. We carried his poor, battered, emaciated body out into the backyard and the Japanese gave us two straw vegetable bags which we pulled over the top and lower halves of his body and sewed them up. I heard later that some men from another cell were taken out that night to the Kiangwan district, where they dug a shallow grave and buried the remains of yet another victim of Japanese "culture."

Before Vong died, other things had been happening. Pop Fleming, who had come into the cell on the same day as myself, had been steadily becoming weaker and weaker. I have never seen a man collect so many lice on his person as he did. One day Ali and I having nothing to do, made a determined attempt to get rid of some of them for him. Pop's glasses had been taken away from him and without them he was practically blind. We got him to peel off his shirt and we carried out an offensive on the unwanted guests. We must have killed more than 500. After we had more or less cleared up his shirt, we started in on his under shirt. We just picked and squeezed, picked and squeezed, for the best part of an hour, but at the end of that time there appeared to be as many lice remaining as there were when we started so we suggested that we ditch the under shirt, as if he continued to wear it, the lice would probably eat him alive. Pop wisely agreed, so we dumped the under shirt into the lavatory. Whilst on the subject of lice, the Japanese occasionally used to pass in a small glass bottle in which they requested us to dump samples of the lice we had on our bodies for examination by their medical staff.

After Vong's death. Pop rapidly began to go down. He was developing a particularly vicious type of sprue and being in such a weakened state, he had great difficulty in making his way to the lavatory. The consequence can well be imagined. The poor old chap was in a filthy state and despite his many pleas to the Japanese to obtain for him a change of clothing from his residence, he never got these. Though the weather was getting very cold, he was still wearing the shorts he came in to Bridge House with. He was constantly getting into trouble with the guards as I don't think he could properly realize that he was in prison, and was always asking the Japanese guards for more tea. He invariably got a crack on his head with a stick, but he never really did learn. He had another bad habit and that was whispering out aloud. He could not whisper softly. This would not only get him into trouble, but the rest of us as well, and the whole cell was at times made to kneel on the floors for a couple of hours as punishment for talking.

Towards the end of November, he began to have periods of semi-consciousness. Finally, Ali who had been taken upstairs for some reason or another remarked to the Japanese that he thought that Pop was dying. They all came rushing down and found the old man lying in a state of semi-consciousness. They ordered him to stand up, which of course he could not do, but still they thought he was shamming and they ordered me to lift him to his feet which I did. Then they told me to stand away from him. As soon as I let him go, he started to collapse. I caught him again before he hit the floor. They hurriedly told me to lay him down and then they all ran out of the cell in a state of excitement. They were so excited that they even forgot to close the door of the cell. I took advantage of this to nip out and have a quick talk with a friend in the next cell. They came back again in about ten minutes with a stretcher on which they placed old Fleming and that was the last we saw of him. We asked about him a week later and were told that he was getting on fine. After the war I learned that they had taken him to the place where he had been living before his arrest and that he had died there three days later. Yet another victim of Japanese "culture."

CHAPTER VI
THE JAPS GET THEIR CONFESSION

MANY things had been happening during this period. People were constantly coming and going. Some Chinese would be brought in for a few days for questioning and would then be suddenly released. We had a few Japanese join us as well and we noticed that they were just as badly treated as we were, except that they were allowed the privilege of leaving the cell every night at eight o'clock for ten or fifteen minutes to have a smoke.

They were also given the privilege of having a bath every ten days. The rest of us never got a bath. Sometimes we were not even permitted to have a wash, but the Japanese prisoners were always permitted this privilege, but should they infringe the rules in any way, they were also given a beating. Most of the cases were those of Japanese who had pulled off some fraudulent deal with regards to the transit of goods in the occupied area. Their usual sentence was "banishment from China to Japan for three years!" This implied that life in Japan was very much tougher than it was in China! They were usually kept in Bridge House until a ship was available for their transportation from China to Japan.

We had one young Japanese interpreter and he had been charged with the rape of a Chinese girl in Nanking. This may sound strange for a people who were constantly committing this crime against the conquered Chinese, but as explained by this particular culprit it turned out that the girl on whom he had forced his unwanted attentions turned out to be the girl-friend of a rather high ranking Japanese officer! Had he not made this "mistake" nothing at all would have happened, as all Chinese girls were considered fair prey by the victorious conquerors. This Jap was a queer individual and was constantly trying to figure out a way to commit suicide. He tried on several occasions to get hold of a glass bottle with which I suppose he intended to use to cut his wrists open. He was wearing a celluloid collar. This collar he broke up into small pieces and swallowed the lot, but he seemed to thrive on this particular diet!

His next trick was to try and throttle himself with a sweat rag and I have seen him twist the sweat rag around his neck and pull it tight and keep it tight until he fell over unconscious. Knowing that we would be visited with terrible punishment if he succeeded in achieving his aim, the rest of us prisoners reported the matter to the guards They came into the cell and gave him a good beating and then proceeded to remove everything from him with which he could have committed suicide. He became quite docile after that and even friendly. He appeared to be quite well-known to the guards and they would stand there talking to him for hours, even late into the night. He was taken out of the cell one day and did not return until bed time. When he came in, it was very obvious that he was as drunk as a fool. He told us that he had been taken out to a Sukiyaki joint, where he had had a rip snorting time and had drunk large quantities of saki. Three days later he left for Japan.

We had another prisoner who had been a Gendarmerie interpreter at Nanking. He had been caught putting the "squeeze" on some of the prisoners there. He was a Formosan, and after his dismissal from the Gendarmerie service was being sent back to Formosa. He knew all the tricks of the trade and even managed to smuggle a packet of cigarettes and some matches into the cell. He was a most welcomed inmate! It was very amusing how we would arrange to have a smoke. The cigarette and matches were cleverly concealed in the cell near the lavatory, which the Japanese used to avoid like plague. When we decided to have a smoke we would all get up and start in marching around the cell.

One of the inmates, a Chinese named Ling Dah, who was a really tough individual, was pretending to be sick. He was therefore allowed to keep two blankets with which to cover himself during the day. Normally all blankets were removed after we got up in the morning. As soon as we got the parade started, a cigarette would be passed to Ling Dah, who cleverly made a cigarette holder out of paper and would then light the cigarette. One at a time, we would drop out of the line and take a good pull at the cigarette and would hold it as long as we could and then blow the smoke up towards the ceiling in the darkest corner of the cell. Needless to say, this one good "drag" would make us as dizzy as the devil. The ashes were all carefully collected and the match stick broken up into tiny bits and disposed of in the lavatory bucket.

This Formosan was full of interesting stories about his experiences with the Gendarmerie and would entertain other prisoners for hours on end with his tales. He had them so interested one day that they did not notice the approach of one of the guards. I was standing up against the bars, when I caught sight of a booted foot coming around the corner. I snapped my fingers, which was the danger signal and the whispering instantly stopped. The guard dashed around and saw the circle of Chinese. He opened the cell door and beckoned to one of the Chinese to come out. This was a little rat named Chen, who had never yet received any ill-treatment, because he had squealed on some of his pals. He promptly got to his feet and pointed to me and said, "Mr. Gendarme, it was not me that was talking, it was that foreigner."

The Gendarme, however, took him outside and gave him a bit of a pasting. He then got me out and despite my protestations that I had not been talking and that Chen had been lying, he made me stand to attention and then started battering me across the face and head with a heavy felt slipper. I did not know that felt could hurt so much. However, I had pretty well got used to pain by that time and managed to stand the beating without yelling.

This seemed to infuriate the swine, because he dropped the slipper and, using the American expression, "Tuffu guy," pulled off his heavy leather belt and pitched into me with that. God, what a beating he gave me, and I certainly yelled then with the pain. He hit me about sixty to seventy times across the face and head. At times I threw up my hands to protect my face, but he was always too quick for me. The final blow was when he turned the belt and struck me with the edge of it across the top of the head. I nearly went down, but remembered in time that if I had gone down, he would have probably started on me with his boots. He did not hit me any more, but again made me stand to attention and bow to him and say in Japanese, "yosh," which means "good," after which he booted me into the cell. As soon as he had disappeared, I jumped on Chen and got him by his throat. If ever I had murder in my heart, it was then as I fully intended killing the little rat. The other Chinese in the cell managed to pry my fingers loose and then as he started to yell, one of them clapped his hand over his mouth and told him that if he squealed on me, they would kill him. Needless to say, we never had any more trouble with Mr. Chen.

About that time we had a new Russian prisoner join us who had just left hospital after an operation for double hernia. Four days after his admission, he was taken up for questioning. I was up on the same day on a day-long questioning bout and saw them torture him for three-quarters of an hour with electricity. His screams were horrible, and I thought that he must have burst the hernia that he had been operated on for. Luckily for him, the electrical gadget which they used, broke down. At the same time he had fainted and he looked so ghastly that they were a bit scared of going on with the torture in another form. He was only with us for about twenty days and was then released. He was in a pretty shaky state when he left, but I heard later that he had recovered.

During my questioning periods, I witnessed many occasions of prisoners getting the "works." On one occasion they brought in four well dressed Chinese, obviously of the business man class, and without even stripping them of their effects, ran them straight up the stairs and started going to town on them. One big fellow after having been severely punched around by a Jap named Tomura, who was a Sergeant Major, was made to hold a heavy bench over his head at arm's length. A Korean gendarme named Shudo stood behind him with a long and heavy piece of wood. Every time the victim's arms began to wobble and the bench was lowered, Shudo would hit him a terrible blow with the stick. This went on until the poor wretch could stand it no longer, and dropped the bench on to his own head. He collapsed unconscious on the floor. Shudo turned around to me with a grin on his face and said, "This bastard killed a man."

In the meantime his companions were being put through various forms of torture. They were all eventually placed in different cells, but about two weeks later, the Japanese found that they had made a mistake and released all four of them!

Another man I saw being tortured with the water cure, beatings and being kicked between the legs who finally admitted that he was a Major in the Fourth Route Army. Later he asked me in the cell what a Major was! He was actually a fish monger in the Foochow Road market. He and his friends had been informed upon falsely by a rival fish selling company, and had been arrested and thrown into Bridge House on this ridiculous charge. He and his pals were still there after I had left and I never knew what eventually happened to them. They were probably all shot.

What finally broke me down was this. One night I was taken out for questioning and after the usual face slapping, kicks, punching, they said that I had better admit my crimes or I would be sorry for it. I just kept reiterating my first statement that I was innocent and that I did not know what I could possibly be considered guilty of. They all suddenly went quiet, and one of them walked out of the room downstairs. I was wondering what was coming next, when suddenly I heard a terrible scream come from downstairs, and a voice in Russian saying, "I do not know, I do not know."

I recognized my friend T's voice and realized that the swine were subjecting her to torture. Later I found out that they had strapped electrodes to her hands and then turned on the juice. Scream after scream rent the air until I could stand it no longer. I made a break for the door, but was tripped up by one of the Japanese and the rest of them jumped on me. Jimmy Yokomizo, the interpreter, yelled at me, "Confess you damn fool and nothing more will happen to her." I then gasped out, "All right, all right, anything you say."

One of them shouted down the stairs and the screaming stopped, but I heard poor T moaning for a long time afterwards. They then produced a lot of documents which they told me to sign.

I replied that I would only sign them on condition that they release T, and that I could guarantee her innocence with my life, and was even prepared to sign a document to the effect that should they discover that T had been guilty of any subversive action against them, that I was prepared to forfeit my life. They went into a long confab about this and one of them left the Office. This was Yokohata. He returned about fifteen minutes later with a keen faced Japanese whom I was told was the Commanding Officer of Bridge House. Later I learnt that his name was Major Nagata. I had seen this man once before and that was when Vong was dying, and Nagata and a group of high ranking Japanese officers were carrying out an inspection of the prisoners. Vong sank to his knees behind the bars and begged for his life. Nagata looked at him as did the highest ranking officer present. The big shot turned around and asked Nagata what it was all about. Nagata shrugged his shoulders and made some reply, laughing as he did so. The big shot then waved his hand at Vong and used the expression, "Bakaranei," which I believe means, "Fool," and laughingly turned on his heel and walked away.

This "gentleman" was now standing before me looking me up and down. Jimmy then turned around to me and said, "Do you mean it about everything. Your life as guarantee for T's innocence?" I replied "Yes."

My reply was passed on to Nagata. Nagata stood there looking at me for some time and then for some unaccountable reason came up to me and put his hand out and shook hands with me and said "Yosh." I turned around to Jimmy and asked him what that meant. He said that Major Nagata had agreed to accept my offer and would order the release of T within a few days. He said, furthermore, that this was a promise on the honour of a Japanese soldier. I then signed whatever they put before me. I told myself that what I was signing meant nothing as it was a case of force majeure, and I signed with my tongue in my cheek. They led me back to my cell and as I passed through the Office, I saw poor T crumpled up in her chair. One electrode was still attached to her hands. A few minutes after I had returned to my cell, I saw them carry T past and heard her being pushed into her own cell which was next to mine. One of the prisoners in the next cell whispered to me after the guards had gone, "Don't worry old man, we will look after her." This was on the 6th December.

At about one o'clock on the 13th December, Nakatani, the Russian speaking Gendarme, swaggered past my cell and grinned at me and said in broken English, "T go home." My heart leapt with joy and a little while later, I heard him say the same thing to T in Russian. I heard her scream with joy and then she asked about me and he replied, "Not yet." They brought her out of the cell with all her belongings and permitted her to say "goodbye" to me. She whispered to me that she would get news to my family of how I was through the Swiss Consular Officials and furthermore, that she would try and get some decent food into me. She was led away crying with happiness.

I was terribly happy and relieved about her release as I realized that had she remained much longer it would have meant the end of her. She was frightfully thin and though 5' 8" in height, only weighed a little over 80 lbs when she left. Two days before her release, Shura obtained her freedom. The Japs came down for her and told her to come out of the cell. She was in a terribly weakened state and could hardly stand. She whispered to me, "This is the end. They are now going to kill me." I told her not to be ridiculous, but she was so terror stricken that she could not stand up and I had to pick her up and carry her out of the cell. Two of the Japs then supported her as she stumbled away. I heard later that it was necessary for her to spend nearly three months in hospital to recuperate, Her husband, who was in the next cell, expressed his joy to me, when he heard of his wife's release.

The following Sunday, December 20th, being my birthday, T obtained permission to send me in a food parcel. This was handed to me on the Saturday. Other friends had chipped in and sent me some good things to eat. I had almost forgotten that such good food could have existed and the sight of so much quite overcame me. Needless to say, I shared with my less fortunate fellow prisoners. A couple of days later, the Japs surprised us all by asking us whether we would like to have our friends send in food parcels on the 24th or 25th. We all agreed on the 25th, Christmas Day. We eagerly looked forward to Friday, and when Friday did come, even though we were behind prison bars, a little of the spirit of Christmas entered into the dingy place. I don't think Bridge House had seen so much good food in its whole existence as a prison. My own parcel was absolutely an "eye opener."

All of us simply gorged ourselves on the good things that were sent in, but we did plan at the same time, that we would pool our food and make it last as long as possible. So on Saturday morning, we only had a tin of sausages. At about eleven o'clock, some of the higher officers came around and looked over the parcels of food that were hanging on pipes outside of the cell, to keep them away from the rats, and began asking to whom each parcel belonged.

Having been informed of the ownership, they wrote our names in Japanese on a piece of paper and tucked the names into each packet. They went around to all the cells and did this and then to our utter horror, they collected all the parcels and took them away. We nearly forgot the punishment that might have resulted through raising a rumpus, but a rumpus we raised. The guards came around with sticks and hit us over our heads and told us to be quiet. That was the last we saw of our Christmas food parcels. In explanation of their action, the Japanese said that a high-ranking officer was inspecting the prison on Monday and therefore the parcels could not be left for him to see.

Sure enough on Monday, there was a terrific "wind up" in Bridge House. Certain of the Chinese prisoners were taken out of the cells and made to wash down the corridors and clean the windows. At half past nine, we were ordered to sit in rows on the floor and they dared us to move an inch. We sat like this until half past eleven, when suddenly there was a terrific amount of shouting and in came the big shots. They were accompanied by Nagata. They walked slowly past the cell and on seeing us white people, dirty, unkempt, unshaved and unwashed, grinned as though highly amused. The inspection took about another half hour, but owing to the fact that the General, or whoever it was, was inspecting the whole of Bridge House, we did not get our food, what there was of it, until three o'clock in the afternoon, and when we did get it, we found that the rations had been cut by half. We did, however, receive normal rations that evening.

In the meantime, we had been joined by a Russian lad, Bob F, who had been transferred to us from another cell. Why we didn't know. He was a good companion and well up to all the tricks of prison life, that is to say, smuggling cigarettes in and matches and various other contraband without being caught. He could also speak a little Japanese and appeared to be a favourite amongst the guards. He was a useful person to have about.

On the night of 28th December, the Japanese from the Office suddenly came in and started in rounding up various people from the different cells. Amongst them were Ali and Bob from our cell. We knew that something big was afoot. They did not return until about half past ten. I was still awake when they came in and they told me that the Japs had been very kind to them, but that they feared that this did not bode well for them. They had been shown their private effects and asked to check them over and when they did so, they were told that all their effects would be handed over to their nearest relatives.

Bob had asked one of them what this was all about, and he was told that he would soon find out. Both Ali and Bob believed that they were for court martial and were going to be shot. They did not like the bit about having their effects handed over to their relatives. At half past five the next morning, there was a terrific hullabaloo and the place appeared to be filled with heavily armed Gendarmes. They began to call out names, and, surrounding the people whose names were called as they came out of the cell, they marched them out. In the dim light of the early morning, I saw them being loaded into trucks. I saw Ali get into the same truck as his beloved Betty, about whom he put his arms. There were several women amongst those who were being taken away.

The cell seemed very empty without my two pals, as I was now the only foreigner left. I thought I had seen the last of them, but about eight o'clock in the evening, I heard trucks being driven into the yard and after much shouting, some of those who had left in the morning came back. The first one to come in was a chap we called Rosy. His face was deadly pale and as he passed our cell I whispered, "What happened Rosy?" The reply was, "Terrible, terrible. I am afraid we are all going to be shot. "

My heart sank to the bottom of my boots. However, a few minutes later, I was glad to see the faces of Bob and Ali. Bob came up to the bars and quickly slipped in a packet of cigarettes and a box of matches, which I promptly passed to Ling Dah, who immediately did the necessary with them in our old hiding place. Bob and Ali came in and I asked Bob what it was all about. He also was terribly shaken and said that he believed that they were going to be shot. Ali, overhearing this, said in a furious voice, "Don't be a bloody fool. I know you are not, because I have just been sentenced to eight god damn years for nothing." I have never seen such a look of relief cross a man's face as that which crossed Bob's. He looked positively happy.

All then gave us a description of the day's proceedings. They had been taken to the Military Headquarters at Kiangwan, where the men had been separated from the women and taken into a big room. There they had been told to strip absolutely naked. A Doctor, or someone like a Doctor, had then come in and had carefully examined every prisoner from head to foot, taking notes of any scars, birthmarks and of any dental work that they had had done. The women had been put through a similar examination. Then they were told to dress again and were permitted to sit on some benches at a table. A more kindly Jap guard than the rest, brought them in some sweet cakes and some tea, as they had had no food since the previous night.

At about ten o'clock, they were all marched in to what appeared to be a court room. There were three judges presiding over the trial and there appeared to be only one defence lawyer. All the charges were read in Japanese, but were not interpreted. The names of all prisoners were called out. When this had been done, they were all marched out again, and one by one were readmitted to the courtroom. An interpreter, whose English was appallingly bad, asked each prisoner if he had anything to say, but as soon as the prisoner opened his mouth to say something, one of the judges motioned to him to be silent. A lot of cross talk went on in Japanese, none of which was understood by the prisoner, and at the end of about ten minutes, the prisoner was marched out and another one admitted.

This went on until all the prisoners had been examined. They were then all marched in again, and the interpreter was ordered by the judge to tell them that they had all been sentenced to death. The female prisoners had screamed and one fell down in a faint.

They were dragged to their feet and ordered to be silent. The one who had fainted had been revived by having some medicine poured down her throat. After a silence of about two minutes, the judge ordered the interpreter to tell the prisoners that though the death sentence had been recommended and passed, that the court had decided to deal leniently with them, to show them how merciful the Japanese could be. He told them that the principle prisoner, a Russian, had been sentenced to ten years imprisonment, the next one, Ali, had been sentenced to eight years imprisonment and so on down the line, the minimum sentence handed out being three years. Two of the prisoners had been sentenced to five years imprisonment, but this sentence was suspended for two years, and that they would be released.

They were asked if they had anything further to say. The Russian lad, who had been sentenced to ten years, then began a vigorous protest, saying that he was of semi-diplomatic standing and that though he had confessed to espionage, that the confession was not true, it having been wrung out of him by repeated torture. Ali said something of the same, as did the others. Their statements were listened to in silence, and on the conclusion of the statements made, the judge through the interpreter told them that their pleas would be considered, and that they would be informed of the final decision of the court within twenty-four hours. They were then marched out. The group that Bob was in had not been tried, as there had not been enough time, but they were told that their trial would take place the next day. After the war, I discovered that their trial had been similar in every respect to the one held the previous day.

The next morning, all those who had been tried and were to be tried, were taken away again at half past five. That was the last I saw of them. Among the second group there had been several acquittals and suspended sentences. This I learned after the war was over. Bob was one of the lucky ones and was back in his home before night fall that night.

CHAPTER VII
A GENTLEMAN INTERPRETER

AS New Year time is a great holiday for the Japs, they seemed to suspend all operations. There were no new prisoners coming in, no releases and no questioning. On New Year's Day, the Japs, to prove how kind and generous they were, came around and gave each prisoner an orange! They told us to eat the oranges and they would be around later to collect the peels and pips. When they came around later, there were neither peels nor pips to be collected, as we had eaten the lot! I did not know that orange peel could be so appetizing.

About this time, a new interpreter had come in whose name was Miyabe. He was a real gentleman and I mean this. He was a Christian and behaved like one and he saved me from many a beating. On one occasion, I had been called out about eleven o'clock one night and asked some questions about a certain telephone number. I was asked, "Do you know this telephone number?" Knowing full well that they knew that I knew, I said "Yes."

"Where is this telephone situated now?"

I replied quite truthfully, "I don't know, I believe somewhere in Nanking Road."

"How can we find out?" I was asked.

I replied, "If you go to the Telephone Company and see Mr. Koshino, he will get hold of the card and give you the information you require." The interpreter was none other than Jimmy Yokomizo! I was then allowed to return to my cell.

Three nights later, I was awakened in the usual manner, that is, by poking a bamboo stick in my back and was told in a gruff voice, "Come." I knew by the tone of the voice that I was in for a bad time. I entered the Office and saw the usual gang sitting around, with the exception of Yokomizo, who had been replaced that night by Miyabe. Miyabe, smiling at me, invited me to come in and sit beside him. When I was seated, he dropped his handkerchief on the floor and as he bent down to pick it up he said, "Don't be nervous." He then straightened up and said, "Mr. Tim, these gentlemen," waving to them, "are very annoyed with you as you have caused them considerable embarrassment. You told them a few nights ago, that if they went to the Telephone Company and saw Mr. Koshino, that he could tell them all about the 9.15 Club. Is that correct?"

"That is absolutely a misstatement. I never said anything of the sort," I said.

Nakatani was sitting on the other side of the desk from me and asked in Japanese what I said. Miyabe replied that I had denied this. Nakatani let out a roar and yelled "Bakaranei" and swung at me with a kendo stick. I just ducked in time to avoid receiving a terrific blow across the face. Miyabe jumped up and stood between me and Nakatani.

After having quietened the rat down, he turned around and asked me what I had said and I told him. He then burst out laughing and turned around and faced the assembled "gentlemen." Their expressions changed from scowls to half grins and they all began asking him what I had said. I don't know what he told them but I heard Yokomizo's name mentioned by him. They then all began to laugh and Nakatani who had been ready to murder me a few minutes before, now grinned at me and said, "Oh berry sorry spoir sreep. Yokomizo fooro make mistake. You rike drink?"

I said, "You bet I like drink, but what kind of drink? I no want Hongkew Hooch." He roared with laughter at this.

"No Hongkew Hooch. Good Scotch Whisky. Haigo. Haigo," he said.

He went over to a cupboard and actually did produce a bottle of John Haig whisky and proceeded to pour me out a good four fingers. I drank half of it neat and believe me I needed it. The rest I watered down with hot tea and sugar. It was the last drink of whisky I had for nearly three years. He also produced some food, which, needless to say, I "wolfed" in a few minutes, and then he gave me two or three cigarettes, after which I was permitted to return to my cell.

This just illustrates the unpredictableness of the Japs. You never know where you are with them. One minute they are quite ready to kill you and the next, they are full of kindness and will give you anything. The same is true the other way around, as at times I had thought that I was O.K. and need not have anything more to fear but found myself a little later to be badly mistaken and would receive at the same hands that had shown me kindness, a terrific beating up. I learned then never, never to trust a Jap!

But Miyabe was one by himself. I heard later from others, that he had been equally kind to them. One prisoner, who was a Clergyman, and had suffered considerably. was taken out for questioning one night and before the other Japs had come into the room, Miyabe went up to him and said, "I know what your calling is Mr. H, I also am a Christian. I can assure you that I shall do my best to prevent you from being tortured or ill-treated any more."

He was as good as his word and H was never tortured thereafter. He sometimes used to get me out of the cell and have long discussions with me on the question of treatment of prisoners and suspects. I said things to him that I would never have dared to say to any other Jap. I will always think kindly of Miyabe and hope that he is doing well now. He deserves it.

One of the interpreters was a particularly nasty bit of work named Yamaguchi. He spoke Russian fluently and was therefore the Russian interpreter. His favourite racket was to in some way or the other, put the "squeeze" on the Russian prisoners. One of his tricks was stealing the Russian prisoners' food whenever a parcel came in for one of them. When a man hasn't had a decent meal for some time, his stomach seems to shrink and when he does get a decent meal, he must eat it slowly. If he does not, after a few mouthfuls he feels that he has gorged himself and simply must stop or else be sick. Yamaguchi's trick was to get the prisoner upstairs in one of the cubicles and set his food in front of him. As soon as the man commenced to eat, he would tell him to hurry up and say that he had only five minutes to finish his food. Of course, the unfortunate wretch would try and get down as much as he could, with the result that after four or five mouthfuls, he would, feel sick and would slow up. Yamaguchi would than say that his time was up, and would refuse to allow the man to take any of the food back to the cell with him, telling him that this was against regulations. He would, however, "promise" the man that he would bring him up the next day so that he could finish the food. Needless to say, this "promise" was never kept and the prisoner would never see his food again. Yamaguchi saw to that, as he promptly ate the lot. We found that he was particularly partial to Russian food.

However, retribution was waiting for him and in due course he was caught. It came about like this. One of the Russian prisoners asked Yamaguchi if he could get some extra food. Yamaguchi told him that he would be pleased to buy him food and cigarettes if he would hand over $200. The prisoner told him that he did not have $200. Yamaguchi therefore suggested that he give him a letter to his wife, ordering his wife to hand over the $200. This the prisoner gladly did, thinking that this was in accordance with the usual routine and regulations. Ten days passed and no food or cigarettes were forthcoming. Nakatani happened to be passing the Russian's cell one day and the Russian asked him, "What about my food and cigarettes?" Nakatani yelled back, "Your food and cigarettes?" The Russian then explained that he had given Yamaguchi a letter to his wife requesting her to hand $200 to him, so that Yamaguchi could buy him the necessary comforts.

Nakatani was immediately very interested and taking the man out of the cell, took him up to the Office and closely questioned him about this procedure. Furthermore, he stood the Russian a good feed and gave him some cigarettes. Next morning I was taken into the Office to be asked a few questions and I saw Yamaguchi swagger in. He let out a rapid fire of ohayos (good morning) and then walked to his desk. The chief interpreter was present and was talking to Tomura. He suddenly swung around and barked something at Yamaguchi. I have never seen a man shrivel up as Yamaguchi did. All his swagger and bounce left him in an instant. He came over to Tomura's desk and the chief interpreter shot a lot of questions at him. Yamaguchi was absolutely tongue tied and could do nothing else, but bow, bow and bow. Tomura finally spat something at him and the miserable little rat picked up his coat and hat and literally slunk out of the Office.

A few days later, I saw a mournful procession passing my cell. It was the bold Yamaguchi en route to prison. I saw him go through the usual process of removing his shoes, tie, belt, etc., and believe me, it gave me considerable pleasure. It appears that Nakatani called around to see the Russian prisoner's wife and she told him that she had handed over $200 to a Japanese. She had retained her husband's letter as a sort of receipt. This receipt Nakatani took over and that spelt the end of Yamaguchi's career as a Gendarmerie interpreter. He had taken an active part in the torturing of many Russian prisoners, including my poor friend T. His downfall was therefore all the more pleasing to me.

CHAPTER VIII

THE NEW QUARTERS IN BRIDGE HOUSE

A T this juncture, I should relate some of the many occurrences which in some way relieved the monotony of life in Bridge House. We were not allowed to read, write, smoke, talk or in any way do anything to help pass the time away, but many of the guards afforded us certain amusement. One of them, I remember, was terribly keen on baseball and discovering that I was an enthusiast, he used to spend hours talking to me on the finer points of the game. He proudly informed me that he was the catcher for the Gendarmerie team, and that his team could lick anything from the Japanese Amateurs up to the New York Giants. He vividly described how he had played on that day and he would then ask me my opinion as to what should have been and what should not have been done. He was keen on all athletics and knew the names of many of the world's champions both professional and amateur. He was also keen on boxing and offered to take me out of the cell to have a couple of rounds with him. Not wanting a good trouncing, having had. enough already, I excused myself that I was too weak. He would laugh uproariously about this.

Another one was particularly fond of music. He was a brutal little beast, as I have seen him take a prisoner and beat him unconscious, and a few minutes later would be walking up and down whistling a selection from one of the operas. He would very often come to the cell bars and talk to me about music. After a long conversation with me one day on the merits of some of the composers, he asked me if I knew the "Rast Rose of Summah." I said, "Yes, I do know it very well."

"O.K. you sing," he said, and I was obliged to sing this song to his whistled accompaniment. He then asked me if I knew "Rub's Ordo Sweeto Song," which being translated means "Love's Old Sweet Song." He made me sing this as well. When I had finished this masterpiece, he put his hands through the bars and patted me on the head as if I was a good schoolboy. But he eventually turned out to be a nuisance, as he would get drunk and try to get me out of the cell at two o'clock in the morning to sing with him. However, by playing "possum," I managed to get out of this.

We had another two guards who were twins and you could not tell them apart. The only way we could tell the difference was that one had three stars on his collar and the other had two. "Three stars" was a swine of the first water. Many a time he caught me leaning against the wall of the cell having a little doze. He would make me come to the bars and hit me over the head with a stick and then make me kneel on the concrete floor for a couple of hours. I never saw him smile at all. On one occasion, I was whistling quietly between my teeth and he came around the corner and caught me and made me stand for an hour and a half with my hands over my head.

His brother, however, "Two stars" was quite a nice fellow, and I remember on one occasion being taken out of the cell to eat some food which my friends had sent in to me. I asked the sergeant on duty if I might smoke a cigarette and he barked a most emphatic "No" at me. "Two stars" came strolling around and stood there watching me. He reached into his pocket and pulled out a cigarette, lit it, and blew the smoke at me. I looked at him, grinned, and remarked that it certainly smelt good. With a slow smile on his face, he handed the cigarette to me and told me that he would keep watch while I smoked it. He instructed me to watch him very carefully and that if he stamped his feet, it was a signal for danger and that I must put the cigarette out.

I certainly enjoyed that cigarette and had it out when I heard him stamping up and down. The sergeant came around the corner but I had managed to dispose the smoke and hide the butt. The sergeant told me to hurry up and get back to the cell. "Two stars" stood behind him and winked at me very gravely.

Most of them, unfortunately, were of the brutal type and would take a keen pleasure in inflicting physical and mental torture on us prisoners. We had in our cell a Chinese named Wong, who had a brother in another cell. Neither had seen each other for some two months. One day the guard on duty came over and called out to Wong, "Come here, I have some good news for you." Wong hurried over to the bars, bowing as he went, and stood by waiting for the good news. The "good" news was that Wong's brother had died. Wong stood there in a stunned silence and the tears trickled out of his eyes. The guard was highly pleased with himself, when he saw how his news had been taken, and went away shouting with laughter. A few days after this, Wong himself was released, but what Wong said after the laughing guard had left made me feel sorry for any Jap that would have fallen into his hands after that.

Other guards would deliberately steal our bread and then give us a half ration of rice in its place. I complained about this one day to one of the guards and got a real good beating for my pains. I am afraid that most of the guards were picked because of their sadistic instincts. They were without mercy and always seemed to derive a great deal of pleasure out of inflicting pain and misery on their prisoners. I have seen the self-same men dressed in civilian clothes and they looked to be perfectly responsible Japanese business men. That is one reason why those people who have dealings with the Japanese should not be taken in by their politeness and apparent civility. It means nothing and it costs the Japanese far less.

Just before the New Year, we had a fine old Chinese gentleman by the name of Chow join us. His fifteen year old son and his thirteen year old daughter were brought in at the same time.

He came in the morning but his son and daughter who had come in at the same time were released in the evening. Mr. Chow had been the Treasurer of the Honan Provincial Government in pre-war days. The Japanese treated him fairly well and he was never knocked about at all. They apparently wanted to get some information from him which he was unable to give. They threatened that they would bring his son and daughter in again if he did not spill the beans, but somehow or the other he managed to satisfy them and this threat was not carried out. He was a great comfort to me, as at that time, the only other companions in my cell were Chinese of a very low type. I had nobody to talk to and life became more and more monotonous. Between six and eight every evening, the guards all liked to gather around at the end of the corridor for a smoke and a talk. This gave us prisoners a chance to also have a little talk and to smoke a forbidden cigarette.

Chow and I would get together in the darkest corner of the cell and talk about all sorts of subjects for those two hours which were the fastest passing hours of the day. Chow and I had a little bet with each other. I bet him that he would be out of the place before me and the stake was that if he got out first, he was to send me the biggest apple pie he could find in Shanghai, and if I got out first, I was to see that he got two flasks of soup. You will note that money was of no interest to us. I won the bet, as after eighteen days, he was released. I wondered if he would remember his promise. He did, and in due course, I did receive a simply huge apple pie.

On January 16th, the Japs came in one evening and called my name out and told me to collect all my stuff together. A wave of joy surged through me as I thought my release was coming. However, no such luck, for on arriving at the Office I was informed that I was to be transferred to another prison which was located among some Chinese houses on the other side of the compound. I was told that it was much cleaner over there and that I would be able to have a bath. At that time I had not had a bath for a hundred and two days! I was pretty filthy! I was taken over to my new quarters and again put into cell number three. There was a pal of mine already in there and for ten days he had been all alone. We shall call him Jimmy. He was frantically glad to see me and kept shaking my hand, until I told him to lay off. He told me that he had been brought from what was known as the Haiphong Road Camp. This camp had not been in existence at the time of my own arrest, but had been opened on the 5th November. He said that they had pulled him out and brought him to Bridge House to question him about the XCDN Radio Station, a station operated by the British Government in Shanghai, prior to the outbreak of hostilities.

He said that the Japs had not beaten him up in any way but looking at his face, which was all puffed up, I recognized signs of beri beri, a disease caused by a lack of vitamin B. I asked him if he had been eating his bread ration and he said that he had not, as by foregoing the bread, he was able to get two rations of rice. Polished rice contains no vitamin B, hence the beri beri. I told him that he was a damn fool and that he must stop the rice immediately and take the bread ration instead, even though it meant less in his stomach.

Jimmy told me that he had managed to smuggle a lot of cigarettes into the cell and that they were hidden under the lid of the trap door over the lavatory hole. On the same evening who should be brought into the cell, but my friend Mr. Yamaguchi, the ex-interpreter! He was only a little fellow when he went in, but he had shrunk considerably during his incarceration. He told us that he knew it was bad in Bridge House, but not as bad as that. He had already received several beatings from his erstwhile companions. Needless to say, he got very little sympathy from me, but what Jimmy and I were worrying about was "Did he smoke?" We sounded him out and he told us that he would sell his soul for a cigarette.

Lighting a cigarette in cell number three in the new section was a different proposition to doing likewise in the old prison. Cell number three was located right in front of the sergeant's desk! The way we used to wangle it was like this: I would place my blanket over my shoulders and stand right in front of the sergeant and start in doing a double mark time. The noise of my feet on the floor boards, drowned out the sound of the striking of the match. Jimmy would get way back to the farthest corner and putting a blanket over his head, would proceed to light the cigarette. As soon as it was lit, he would cough. He being the lighter, would get the first smoke, while Yamaguchi and the Chinese named Ghen Pao Ling and I would keep our eyes on the sergeant of the guard. Jinmy would have three or four good "drags" and then the next one would go over and have his turn. The smoker kept the lid of the lavatory open and at the same time kept a small piece of paper in his hands 'with some saliva in it so as to ensure the rapid quenching of the cigarette in the event of an alarm. The ashes, match stalk, etc., were disposed of down the lavatory. We smoked an average of ten cigarettes a day there!

Though I was supposed to get a bath after my admission to the new section, I never did get one, because as luck would have it, the Japanese bath had broken down. In one way this was a blessing in disguise, as I noticed that all the prisoners who had had baths suffered very badly from colds. I never had a cold the whole time I was there. One of the advantages of being at the new prison was that we did get ten minutes exercise every day. The guards, however, were much stricter and not a day passed, but that some prisoner received a good beating for some infringement or other of the rules. Five days after my admission there, Jimmy was taken out and sent back to Haiphong Road.

There were then only three of us left in the cell, The Chinese Chen, Yamaguchi and myself. The weather at this time was exceedingly cold and to our starved bodies it was absolute torture. We never felt warm and used to envy the Japanese guards sitting around their hibashi or porcelain charcoal burner. The days became most monotonous, as there was little I could talk about to Yamaguchi or Chen. We were supposed as I have already said, to get ten minutes exercise per day, but this depended as to how the guards felt. The exercise consisted of walking around and around a tiny court-yard, but even five minutes of this proved exhausting but we would just keep on going despite our tiredness, as if we stopped, we were immediately pushed back into the cell, and we did not want to miss a minute of this precious exercising time.

Two Chinese girls had been brought in and had been in for about five days. One of them decided that she had had enough of it and she managed to literally cry her way out. She howled for two solid days and told the Japanese that she was in great pain. They, of course, would not believe her. They yelled at her, threatened her, gave her a good beating, but found that this only made her worse and finally they got so tired of hearing her shrieks that they released her and her pal. She kept up the howling all the way out and we could hear her cries in the lane outside the courtyard. She was one of the lucky ones and her pal also benefited by her efforts.

On the 26th January, a most interesting prisoner was brought in. A Russian named Y, who was a well-known Shanghai crook. He was an expert forger of signatures and had several years previously defrauded a large company and a bank of a huge sum of money. He was only caught when he tried it a second time. Even though I knew him to be an absolute crook, I could not help liking him. He told me that he had been arrested by the Japanese for having attempted to sell gold coin to the local Italian Consul General. He laughed heartily about this, and said, "As if I had any gold coin, but I did manage to get $143,000 out of the wop Consul!" The funny thing was that the Japanese had pulled him in because they actually believed that he did have some gold coins. They had arrested him and taken him before the Italian Consul, who, to save his own face, had had to deny that he knew him. However, that did not prevent Y being thrown into Bridge House and being subjected to a lot of torture in order to obtain from him the secret of his "golden hoard." He demonstrated to me in the cell how clever a forger he was. He asked me to sign my name using my usual signature. He took one glance at it, turned the bit of paper over and very expertly duplicated it.

He was an old gaolbird and told me not to worry if I was sent to the local gaol, as he knew all the warders there, who he said were his friends. He said, at the time, that he expected to be out of Bridge House within a week or so, and that if and when I was sent to Ward Road prison, I was to tell Warder so and so that I was a friend of his and to go and see him on my behalf, and that he would keep me well supplied with cigarettes and other comforts. He assured me that he would not do me in the eye, as there is a certain honour between gaolbirds! It was a good job that I did not have to depend upon his generosity, as I later discovered that he spent seven months in Bridge House and was taken out and released in a pitiful condition.

CHAPTER IX
SENT "HOME"

O N the 27th January, I was suddenly taken out of the cell over to the Office. Arriving there I was treated with considerable courtesy and kindness. I found all my personal effects laid out on a desk and was told to check everything over to see that there was nothing missing. At first my hopes of release soared to the very skies, but I suddenly heard the words, "Do not worry, this property will be looked after." It immediately flashed through my head that I was to be sent the next day to Kiangwan for court martial. Having checked over my stuff and noted the articles missing, which included a gold ring and my movie projector, I was taken back to the cell. On the way over I asked my escort in a mixture of Japanese and Chinese what they were going to do with me the next day. He merely laughed and shrugged his shoulders and said, "I don't know." I saw some of my other companions on their way over and presumed that they were going for a similar purpose.

When I got back to the cell I was too upset and, to be frank, too scared to do much talking with my fellow prisoners, but took to pacing up and down the cell like a caged animal, figuring out what I was going to say the next day at the court martial. I was determined to expose the hideous tortures I had been subjected to and to say that whatever I had signed had been signed under duress. I quite realized that it probably would not do me much good, but that at least it would give me the satisfaction of speaking my mind.

At five o'clock In the afternoon there was a great commotion and a huge number of prisoners were brought in, and looking through the bars, I recognized several of my old pals and fellow cell mates from the other block. After much shoving and shouting some of them were pushed into my cell. We greeted each other like long lost brothers. Amongst them was my friend D, who was supposed to be connected with me in the matter of "espionage." We immediately got together in a corner and started in exchanging notes. He told me that he had also been taken over to the Office and made to sign for his personal effects and he realized that it did not look so good.

After we had been talking for some time, one of the Gendarmes named Shudo, a Korean, unlocked the door of the cell, came in and shouted out, "Is anybody in here in the same case?" Both D and I looked blank and innocently at him, pretending that we did not know whether we were in the same case or not. Shudo was, however, not to be bluffed, and he said, "You two are in. You," pointing at me, "come out." I collected my few belongings and followed him out. It appeared that I was connected with someone in each of the cells with the exception of the women's cell. He grinned at me and said, "Can I trust you with these five beautiful girls?" I replied that he could, as what could a bloke do, who had been in Bridge House 113 days? He laughed and pushed me in with the women.

There were five of them there and conditions were fairly cramped, as we were in a cell 8' x 8'. Four of the women were of the ordinary class, but the other was a perfect little lady named Lily K. She could speak English fluently and also several Chinese dialects. Being so intelligent, the Japs had figured out that she must be a spy. She had already been in nearly four months, but the Japs had not been unduly cruel to her and she was still in fairly good shape. As these women had never had a man in the cell with them before, we had all the awkward and embarrassing business to go over again about the use of the lavatories, etc. However, I assured them, through Lily, that I had been a prisoner too long to worry or notice anything like that and they were to take no notice of me.

About half past six, a very frightened Chinese male was pushed into the cell. He sat there as I had done 113 days before, too terror stricken to talk or even think. I eventually got him to tell me his name and he informed me that he was a student and had been arrested at his University on the eve of his departure for home at the time of the Chinese New Year holidays. As usual, he had no idea why he and his two friends had been arrested. Poor fellow, he was soon to discover what Bridge House meant because shortly after seven, they took him out. He was handcuffed and chained and led off crying softly to himself.

About two o'clock in the morning, I was awakened from my sleep by the sounds of crying and moaning and the rattling of the key in the lock. The student had returned and he was a pitiful looking sight. He was unable to walk and just lay across the floor. He appeared to be soaking wet and I noticed that there were some snow flakes in his hair. He was shivering with cold and terror. I dragged him over to my bed, covered him with my blankets and lay down beside him to warm him up. He tried to talk to me, but I told him to save it for the morning. He appeared to be in great agony and cried for the rest of the night.

Dawn eventually broke and I was fully expecting to hear the tramp of the guards coming in to take my companions and me to Kiangwan for the trial, but nothing eventuated, and at the usual hour of half past six, the guards came around with their "Sho, sho" which was their signal to "Rise and shine." I could see that it had been snowing all night and it was bitterly cold. The student was unable to move, so I dragged him into the corner. He told me that someone had given information against him and his two friends, that they were connected with the Chungking Underground Movement. When he denied it, they had subjected him to some terrible tortures, the worst one being that of having his posterior bared and roasted with lighted newspapers, after which they plunged him stark naked into an ice cold bath of water.

They had also burnt the bottoms of his feet and the rest of his body was a mass of bruises. His buttocks and the soles of his feet were a shocking sight and they appeared to be one big blister, the surrounding flesh also being blackened and scorched. I asked him if he had admitted anything and he had replied that he had not. I tried to reassure him by saying that as he had had one dose, they would not do it to him again.

The Japs would not let any of the men out for a wash, so I had to stay dirty, but Lily took a handkerchief out for me and brought it back wet, so at least I had a bit of a clean up before, as I thought, I was taken out to Kiangwan. The morning passed slowly and nothing happened. At mid-day, we got our usual bowl of rice and sip of tea. I then figured out that because of the inclement weather the trial had been postponed. About 1.30, three of the office men came in with some slips of paper in their hands and started in calling out the names. My name was among those called. They told us to take all our stuff and stand in a row. I said goodbye to Lily and she told me not to worry, and that being a Christian, she would pray for my safety. She felt sure that no harm would come to me.

There were nine of us standing in the corridor with our bundles over our shoulders. There was much counting of noses and roll-calling, and once they were satisfied, we were told to follow our escort. D and I slipped up beside one of them and asked him where we were going. He grinned at us and said, "Home." Knowing the Japs' peculiar sense of humour, I did not believe him. However, when we arrived at the Office, Jimmy Yokomizo greeted us by saying, "Will you please place your effects in the corner near the front door gentlemen!" Gentlemen! I had not been called that for a long time, but I was not being fooled.

Tomura and a few others were also present. My name was called out and I stepped forward to the desk. On it were lying all my personal effects. I was told to check it over and having done so was stepping back again, when they told me to take it as it was mine. I cannot tell you how I felt with my wrist watch on once more, the tie around my neck and my pockets with things in them. One by one the same was done with the rest. We were then told to pay attention to Tomura. He launched out into a long speech in Japanese. When he had stopped talking, Jimmy translated it and it was roughly as follows: "Mr. Tomura says tnat today the 28th January, you should all have been going to Kiang-wan for court martial for the crimes you have committed, but, being kind hearted, he has decided to deal very leniently with you. He has therefore decided to let you go home." We gasped out, all at one time. "Home?"

He turned around and said something to Tomura who replied to him and then continued to us, "No, I am sorry, not home, but to a special camp just like home! where you will be able to see your friends, write letters, play games, have good food and do anything you like. You will be kept there for a little time, until the war is over, but that if you ever commit these crimes again, no mercy will be shown to you. You have therefore to thank Mr. Tomura for his kindness of heart." We faced Tomura and ironically bowed and said "Thank you." The irony went right over his head and he replied in Japanese, "Don't mention it."

We then asked if we might go and see our people and be granted a sort of leave of absence for eight or nine hours, in order to go home, get cleaned up, collect a few of our possessions and then proceed to the camp. We promised that we would not communicate with anyone or in any way divulge anything at all. Tomura stood thinking for at least two minutes, and then slowly shook his head and through . . . . .

(The text is broken here where a page is missing from the original typescript)

. . . . . out. More about my opinions on this later.

CHAPTER X
HAIPHONG ROAD CAMP

THE thrill and joy of knowing that we were still alive and were, we were hoping, seeing the last of Bridge House was indescribable. Though, we were dirty, ragged, unshaven and emaciated, curious spectators could see the looks of joyous excitement on our faces. We were still alive! That was the great thing! Where there is life there is hope! Only one Japanese Gendarme accompanied us on the trip to Haiphong Road and he did not object or attempt to stop us when we waved to people we knew on the streets. Those we did know, looked blankly at us not recognizing us in our filthy state. Some of them recognized us by our voices alone and waved frantically back. It was a great feeling.

We arrived at the Haiphong Road concentration camp on 28th January 1943. It was located in the north western part of the city, and was adjacent to the Headquarters of the then-famous Nagai Wata Kaisha Cotton Mills. The reason for this location being very obvious. The property whereon the camp buildings were located was quite extensive. The camp itself consisted, of two main buildings, one occupied by the Japs and the other by the prisoners. A roadway separated the two buildings. A large, well kept garden lay in front of the buildings and a large plot of ground at the back was devoted to vegetable growing. On the East side of the building was a vacant lot which was used as a sort of recreation ground and playing field. These buildings had originally been built to house a large Chinese family, and in the troublous days of 1927 it had been occupied by the U. S. Marine Corps as a battalion Headquarters, and it had been used as such up to the outbreak of the Pacific war, when the Japs took it over. The whole place was surrounded by a high wall. The entrance lodge had been converted to a guard-house. There were only two sentries on duty, one at the front gate and one at the back. An extra sentry was always on guard when we were playing games.

Our arrival was noted by several of the inmates and the news quickly spread over the building and a crowd of fellows poured out to welcome us. We were taken to the Administration building and there we were made to fill in forms and sign a declaration that we would not attempt to escape. Our effects were then thoroughly searched. The Japs relieved me of all my movie apparatus, which they said would be kept for me "a little time until the war ended." We were then turned over to our own people, who took us to the camp clinic. There we were made to strip off our verminous clothes, which were taken away for the purpose of delousing. Believe me they needed it, as we were all as lousy as coots!

We were then given a thorough medical examination and weighed. My weight was then 147 lbs. When I entered Bridge House I had weighed 190 lbs! Many of our friends rallied around and supplied us with pyjamas and bedding and we were all sent straight in to hospital. Naturally, the first thing we asked for was food, and at that time there was a considerable amount of food available in the camp. The quality was not up to much, but to us famished men, it was better than a dinner at the Waldorf Hotel. Rice and scrambled eggs! Will I ever forget that? Smokes were to be had in plenty, and we smoked until our tongues were burnt raw. The joy of once more being able to lie between clean sheets was indescribable. The bath was marvellous. The first one I had had in 114 days! The hot water and soap stung my skin terribly, but I still enjoyed the sensation immensely.

The camp barber too had a field day, disposing of beards and mops of long uncut hair. We were all given injections of Vitamin

B which we were sorely in need of as a few of us were suffering from Beri Beri, a very uncomfortable and distressing disease. Of course, we just could not sleep that first night. We were not allowed visitors, but we all sat around on our beds, talking, talking and talking. This is the result of not being allowed to talk in prison. We just had to get the steam out of our systems.

Occasionally, one of us would go and lie down and, the sense of relief being too much, it was nothing to see a grown man crying like a child, crying with relief that he was once more safe, or comparatively so. Our own camp representatives and the doctor visited us and listened to the stories of what we had gone

The garden at the Haiphong Road camp

through. I understood later that all our stories had been carefully written down for use at some future date. This was dangerous, as we never knew when the Japs might make a raid and we would get into hot water. We were advised not to talk about our experiences too much with the other members of the camp, as unfortunately there were a few undesirables in the camp. We discovered several later on.

Haiphong Road camp was supposed to be a collection of prominent citizens of Shanghai. At least that is how we were described by the local press when the camp had been opened. Many of the men in the camp had been separated from their wives and children, who later had been interned in other camps. Repeated requests by these men to rejoin their families had been rejected by the Japs, with no explanation given for the action which had been taken. At first, they were told that the matter was under consideration by Tokyo and that may be something would be done. As will be described later, it will be seen that this was never done.

The conditions in the camp at the time of our arrival were very good. Our own. camp representatives and committee had wisely enforced a rule that a large proportion of the comforts money allowed us by our respective governments be used for the purchase of extra food and fuel. Though many grumbled at this seemingly dictatorial action, they learned that our leaders had been far-sighted and that eventually we owed to that foresight our very existence. The first winter we actually had steam heating and hot baths were available every day! Each prisoner received a ration of cracked wheat once a day which went a lot towards counteracting Beri Beri, because of its high Vitamin B content. We were not made to do any manual work by the Japs, but of course, all the duties in the camp had to be carried out by the prisoners themselves.

The majority of us who had been returned from Bridge House remained in hospital for about two weeks, recuperating after our terrible experience, after which we were assigned to various camp duties. None of these duties were heavy as there were plenty of men to carry them out. Our friends on the outside had been notified of our release and immediately gathered together our effects which were sent in to us. Parcels containing foodstuffs were coming into the camp every day from friends, relations and well wishers through the medium of the International Red Cross. The Japanese, of course, thoroughly searched all these parcels and many amusing discoveries were made by them. They discovered that messages were being sent in written on rolls of toilet paper. Thereafter, every roll that came in was most carefully examined.

The prisoners themselves got up to all sorts of tricks to get messages out to their relatives and friends, and though many did get out, the Japanese caught several. At first they merely warned the offenders, but later threatened them with dire punishments, but this, of course, did not stop some of the bolder members. At that time we were also allowed the use of a radio, which only received the local broadcast. This was permitted up to the end of May, 1943, when the tide began to turn, and the Japs did not want us to hear and know too much. We were, however, able to obtain a good idea as to how things were progressing from the one Japanese-English language newspaper permitted.

After my release from hospital, I was assigned to a room with eleven other prisoners. We were very crowded and everybody seemed to get in everybody else's way. This unfortunately led to trouble at times, as was only to be expected when you get a lot of people seeing each other, the same old faces day after day. Once we had settled down, life began to be very monotonous. Many of us had taken up the study of languages and for nearly two years, I persevered with Russian, but I am sorry to say that I did not become very proficient in it. Many, however, learned Chinese, Spanish and French and learned it very well indeed.

After our light duties of the day ended, which was about eight to ten in the morning, we had nothing to do except sit down, read, talk or sleep. Had we been allowed to write long letters, it might have helped, but we were only allowed one letter a month and that, of only 50 words. In addition to the one letter of 50 words a month, we were allowed to send two letters a year abroad consisting of only 25 words. The afternoons were spent in either watching a football or baseball match. This was a great recreation and was much appreciated by all concerned.

The Japs left us alone pretty well, but as time wore on, came to increase their restrictions on us, which made life more and more irksome. There was a roll call morning and evening when the whole camp had to line up by rooms. The inspecting officer, sometimes commissioned and sometimes non-commissioned, would come to each group when the captain would have to call the room to attention and, bowing himself, give his report in Japanese. The numbering was also done in Japanese. One day, they brought out an order that we would all have to bow to the sentries. We first of all ignored this order, but when threatened with punishment, we decided to bow, and how! We assembled ourselves in sections of four and in an endless stream commenced to walk past the lone Japanese sentry. When we got opposite him we would halt, remove our hats and bow. He, of course, had to acknowledge the salute by bowing back to us. After about an hour of this continuous bowing, he yelled out to us to go away and he took himself off into the guard-house to avoid the bowing. This put an effective end to all further bowing.

We had one officer, however, who we referred to as "Dogface" and he was a particularly objectionable brute. He was positively "bowing mad" and whenever it was his turn to call the roll, he would keep us all standing until he had visited every room and made them bow several times. We had to do it by numbers, and his great joy was to walk up to some fellow whose back was humped up like a camel's, and give him a resounding thump. This used to amuse him immensely and he would walk around with a sardonic grin on his face. He was also fond of striking the prisoners and on the slightest excuse would haul off and give you a slap right across your face. Repeated complaints to the commandant failed to stop him.

Visitors' day at Haiphong Road

He was always telling us about how great a samurai or warrior he was and at the slightest excuse would whip out his sword and slice a branch off a tree and would then look around proudly to see whether his prowessness as a swordsman had been noted. He was usually disappointed, as we all made a point of looking the other way. Then to draw attention, he would slice off another branch giving a terrible shout at the same time, but he never got any change out of us. I am quite sure that "Dogface" would cheerfully have cut a few of our heads off, if he had had a chance to do it. My God, how he hated us, and yet despite all his pride, he would not hesitate to ask us to give him some article of our clothing, such as ties and waist-coats. I never saw him wear civilian clothes, but he appeared to be simply mad about ties.

He was a brute to his own men as well, and frequently knocked them about. On one occasion, he had taken half the camp garrison out on a route march. He had evidently made them run the last half mile back as on arrival at the camp, the K.C.O, who was absolutely puffed, was unable to give the necessary orders to "right dress" etc. "Dogface" flew at him and before all us prisoners, he batted him from one end of the parade ground to the other, and finished off by giving him a sound kick in the stomach. Then, pulling down his jacket and assuming a very dignified air, he marched majestically away. We all roared with laughter and he glared furiously at us. He was with us about seven or eight months and on his departure had the audacity to ask the camp for a present. It is hardly necessary to say that he did not get it.

In addition to the ordinary military guards in the camp, we had two gendarmes, two Japanese municipal police and four Indian sikh policemen to guard us. Why the sikh policemen and the Jap municipal police were there, we never discovered. We had an idea that the sikhs were put there in an endeavour to humiliate us. In this way they failed miserably. Most of the sikhs were rather decent fellows and were very sympathetic in their attitude towards us, always addressing us as "Sahib." Others were, of course, pro-Jap, and could never be trusted. Many of them risked severe punishment by taking out messages, and this brings us to the story of tho murder of William Hutton.

CHAPTER XI
THE SAD END OF WILLIAM HUTTON

BEFORE recounting the sad story of William Hutton, I shall give a few more details of what Haiphong Road camp really was. It was in reality a camp for those people who had already fallen foul of the Japanese or against whom the Japanese entertained some suspicion or those whom they thought had at some time or other had some dangerous thoughts. Therefore, an inmate of Haiphong Road never knew when the Gendarme would have him out for special investigation or questioning. Up to the time I became a member of the camp, an average of one or two per week had been taken out for periods varying from ten to forty days. Some of them had returned thinner but otherwise unharmed, whilst others had come back bearing marks of the beast on their bodies, so that every time the "little black car" was seen to come in through the gates, the question was, "Whose turn is it now?"

To give you an idea as to how deep the terror had struck into me, the following incident is illuminating. About six weeks after my entry into camp, I was sitting reading in the library. One of the camp representatives put his head into the door and said, "Mr. Tim, can I see you for a moment outside." I jumped up and went out and he said, "Now keep your hair on and don't get the wind up, but there is a man from Bridge House over at the Administration Building and he wants to see you. He is also asking for K, and K is in the office waiting, so you had better go in there and both of you go over together."

I became absolutely speechless with fear, and began to tremble violently. Pulling myself together, I went in to the Office and saw K standing there, his face absolutely ashen. K turned to me

and said, "My God, can't they leave us alone?" I could say nothing. We both turned around and walked out of the office, but out in the open, we both came to a standstill again and looked at each other in horror. We again got going and walked to the Administration Building.

Camp commandant, Colonel Odera

Outside the door was standing the "little black car!" Arriving at the door of the office, we knocked and then walked in. Standing there was Suzuki, grinning at us! He greeted us by name and asked us how we were and how were our bodies. We both replied that we were not so well. He then said, "Never mind, plenty good food, plenty play, soon be all right."

Honda, the Deputy Camp Commandant said, with a grin, "You know Mr. Suzuki very well I see."

We replied that we did and to ourselves said, "too well." Suzuki said something to him in Japanese and Honda turning around told us that when we had left Bridge House, we had reported the loss of some of the articles which had been confiscated on our arrest. He was pleased to inform me that Mr. Suzuki had recovered my movie projector which had now been returned and would be kept by the camp authorities for safe-keeping, but he regretted that he had so far been unable to find the gold rings which K and I had reported missing.

K and I both grinned broadly and then in our relief hastened to assure Suzuki that it did not matter at all, not one bit, please don't bother any further, that was quite all right etc, etc. Suzuki, however, said, "Japanese army very honest. Those rings must find. Soon will find and will bring to you."

We were then told that we could go and we did not need a second telling. When we got outside, we both found that we had been sweating profusely, so great had been our fright and terror. The end of the story was that about three weeks later, our rings were duly returned to us! Another example of the unpredictability of the Japs and their actions. At times they would cheerfully rob you of everything you had and yet at other times they would go to no end of trouble to see that a prisoner's effects were restored to him.

And now the tragic story of William Hutton. One afternoon at about the end of July, we were all out in the open enjoying the cool evening breezes after an exceedingly hot day. One man whom I shall call "Ginger" was sitting beside one of the paths. About 12 feet away from him there was standing a sikh guard, No.139. His name was Katah Singh. Ginger was apparently reading a book and making some notes with a pencil. Without warning, 139 suddenly ran towards him and, seizing him by the waist band of his trousers, dragged him to his feet and started shouting at him, "I take you Japanese office." At that time, two Japanese sentries passing by on their way to their posts stopped and endeavoured to make the sikh release Ginger.

The sikh, however, refused to do so and shouted something unintelligible and wildly at the Japanese. They both laughed and went on their way. The sikh then dragged Ginger to the Japanese office. He was taken into the office used by the Gendarmerie Section attached to the camp and we saw the doors close, and were unable to see what was going on. He had not been released by roll call time and just after the roll had been called and the prisoners dismissed, the chief camp representative C, came up and shouted out, "Come down Tim and bring your bugle." When I got downstairs, C told me to stand by to blow the "fall in" as there was to be an identification parade.

I strolled out of the building and as soon as I got outside, I was pounced upon by 139, who swung me around so that the light shone on my face. He turned to the Japanese and said, "No blong this man, blong policeman 126." I shook his hand off my arm and told him that I was the bugler and showed him my bugle. The Japanese all laughed. Getting the signal to go ahead, I blew "fall in" and then reported to my own room. I learned later that the sikh went to two rooms, one where he drew a blank and the other where he picked out one of the prisoners whom we shall call Dick. Dick was promptly taken over to the Administration Office by the Japs.

About half past ten that evening, both men were released. I noticed that Ginger had a bruise or two on his face and a cut on the forehead. Dick apparently had not been touched. They both said that the case, as far as they knew, was closed and that the sikh had been proved a liar.

Apparently he had accused Ginger of trying to bribe him to take a message out of the camp. As Ginger had formerly been connected with the Police and knew all the sikhs, it was hardly likely that he would have asked this particular sikh to do him a favour, as he knew him to be a "bad egg." Previous to this incident, the same sikh had been the cause of two American members of the camp, having their faces slapped. Personally, I was not so sure that the case was closed, as the Japs did not so easily let go of anything once they had got their teeth into it. My opinions were quite correct, as the next morning Ginger and Dick were both called for and told to get ready, as they were to be taken out!

A few minutes later, we saw Hutton go to the office and after being closeted with Honda for some time, he came out and said, "Well boys, I'm for it. The little swine won't believe my story."

It transpired that Dick had been pulled into the affair by the sikh, who had accused him of being Ginger's accomplice. As both Dick and Hutton looked a little bit alike, the sikh had got his men mixed up. It seems that Hutton walking past Ginger had asked Ginger how much he wanted for his pencil. Ginger had replied $60, as it cost $70 outside, whereupon Hutton laughingly offered him $10 and then walked on. According to the sikh, this money which was being talked about was the amount of the bribe. Hearing that Dick was to suffer for something that he had not done, Hutton very gallantly went to Honda and told him the whole story. Honda had refused to believe him and had ordered him to go out in Dick's stead. I was standing near the gate as Hutton went out looking healthy and cheerful. He turned around and laughingly said, "Cheerio Tim, don't worry about me. I'll be seeing you."

Ten days went by. During these ten days there had been a typhoon and one of our big trees, later to be known as Hutton's tree, had been blown down and was lying across the main roadway. A bunch of us were working on it trying to get it up, when we saw a car coming in through the gate. Looking at the car, I saw Ginger sitting in the back, alone. Beside the driver in the front seat were two Japs, one a colossal devil. They drove around one of the side paths and stopped in front of our building. I went over to have a look at Ginger and saw that he looked emaciated, exhausted and very dirty. He called out to me, "Tim, go and get the doctor quick."

I promptly ran into the clinic and met Dr. S to whom I passed the message. Dr. S immediately went out and walked towards the car. The big Jap got out and stood in his way and pushing him back said, "No go, you go way." Dr. S stood up to him and replied, "I am the doctor and that man needs me." The Jap then stood aside. I was just behind the doctor when he got to the window of the car and said, "What's the matter Ginger?"

For an answer, Ginger pointed to the bottom of the car. Dr. S. looked down and I saw him give a start. He swung around to me and said, "Tim, get the stretcher and the stretcher bearers, quick!"

Still not knowing what it was all about, I did what I was told. The stretcher was taken to the other side of the car, the door opened, and there lay Hutton! What a horrible sight he looked. He had been beaten and battered to a point almost beyond recognition. One glance showed that he was hopelessly insane. We lifted him out and we could see that his body was a mass of burns and bruises. Some words had been carved into his legs with a sharp instrument. His wrists had been gashed open by ropes and they were already festering sores. He was babbling incoherently.

We rushed him into our clinic where First Aid was applied. In the meantime, Honda had been informed of his return and had hurried over to see him. He actually changed colour when his eyes surveyed the pitiful object lying before him. An American Doctor, Dr. D, glared at him and said, "Honda, I hold you personally responsible for this man's condition." Honda feebly replied, "He struck a Grendarme and they had to tie him up."

Dr. D's reply to this was, "I don't care who he struck. What your people have done to this man is horrible and there is no excuse. I will hold you responsible." Honda muttered something under his breath which sounded like, "I will get high Japanese doctor," and then shuffled out.

Hutton was taken to the isolation ward and was later visited by a very high ranking Japanese medical officer, who after examining him said that he thought in two or three days, he would be all right. During the day he seemed to rally in strength, but not mentally, because he seemed to become more violent and kept screaming out, "Black, white, black, white, up, down, up, down," and then began to scream. It was horrible. The next day in the afternoon, the Jap doctor again visited him and after his visit, it was decided to remove him to a mental home. As he was being carried out, it was quite plain to see that he was a dying man. That evening at nine o'clock a brief notice appeared on the notice board stating that William Hutton had died. Yet another victim of Japanese culture!

CHAPTER XII
A LUCKY FEW HEAD HOME

A WAVE of indignation had swept through the camp against the Japanese and the tree which we had been raising at the time when Hutton was brought back still lay across the roadway. The Japanese issued instructions that we were to carry on with the job of raising the tree, and we had one and all refused point blank. The Japs realized that it would be a mistake on their part to use force, in order to compel us to do the work, so they sent for the camp representatives and informed them that though the affair had been an unfortunate one, what had been done, had been done, and we must realize that we were prisoners and therefore not in a position to refuse to do anything. They said that they wished to avoid any further incidents of any kind and hoped therefore that the men would be sensible. A meeting was held between the camp representatives and the room captains and after some heated discussion, it was generally agreed that there was no sense in running our heads against a brick wall. We therefore turned to and raised the tree with the assistance of every available Japanese soldier. The tree was thereafter named Hutton's tree and stood as a memorial to him.

We were wondering why the Japanese had been so restrained in their dealings with us regarding the raising of the tree and shortly after this incident, the reason was revealed. We had for some time been hearing of a repatriation ship and, of course, we were all hoping that one and all of us would be fortunate enough to be repatriated. However, that good fortune was only to fall to the lot of 43 of us, thirty nine Americans and four Canadians. One of those to be repatriated was Dr. D, who had attended Hutton before he died and we knew that he would not in any way hold anything back when reciting the story of Hutton's death, if he got back to America. Those who were going were told that they would be allowed so much luggage and were told what they could take and what they couldn't take. Arrangements, however, were secretly made to take certain information out and though I never really did learn how and if it was done, a rumour went round that some very valuable documents had been smuggled out in the legs of camp chairs!

We finally learned that the ship was due to leave on the 20th September and great excitement prevailed amongst the fortunate ones. There was much weighing of baggage and disposing of unwanted articles. Many incidents occurred which showed that times of stress very often bring out the worst in a man. Many of those who were fortunate enough to be leaving would not give one item of their unwanted goods to their less fortunate brethren. They tried to exact as high a price as they possibly could, and one Christian gentleman, a missionary, finding that he could not get his price for a deck chair, very systematically and methodically destroyed the article. Such is life.

During the time prior to their departure, the Japs had eased up very considerably with regard to the discipline of the camp. Only three men were taken away in the "little black car." One returned after forty-eight hours with a story which was truly amazing. He said that when he arrived at the former Union Jack Club, which was then used as a Gendarmerie station, he was asked a few inconsequential questions and instead of being made to sleep in the cell, he had been provided with a soft couch in one of the rooms. He had also been given a bottle of beer with his supper, which was a very good and filling one! After supper, the Japs had asked him if he would like to have a walk along the Bubbling Well Road. They took him for quite a long stroll, which he thoroughly enjoyed. It was very obvious that the Japanese

Building in the Haiphong Road camp

were trying to wipe out the memory of Hutton's death in the minds of those who were going away. In this they did not succeed. A week or so later, two more men who were brothers were taken out to the former American School, where they were only kept for twenty-four hours and then returned to the camp. They had in no way been ill-treated.

Eventually, the eve of the great day arrived, and those who were going, were assembled and addressed by Colonel Odera, the camp commandant. Ho told them that he was very happy that they were about to return to their native lands and that he had been very pleased to have such nice people under him. He trusted that they would tell the folks back home that they had been well treated! He finished off his speech by announcing that he was presenting a case of saki to the repatriates, so that they could celebrate before leaving the camp. They celebrated, and how! A grand concert was also held that night, which was attended by all the Japanese garrison.

The next morning, the repatriates were assembled and after saying goodbye to us, they crossed the road and were all lined up on the tennis court. Customs Officers and police appeared on the scene and we witnessed the spectacle of them being searched to the skin. The Japs were certainly making sure that they were not taking anything out that they should not be taking. Each of the repatriates were then handed a rosette which was to be pinned to their coats. Colonel Odera once more addressed them and then went around and shook each one of them by the hand. Very touching indeed! There were many shouts from us of "Don't forget Hutton," and the reply came back, "We won't." They were then marched out to the tune of "Aloha Oe" which was played by our camp band. I may say that many of us had lumps in our throats, as we felt then that it would never be our good fortune to be taking the same route. A cloud of despondency and gloom fell over the whole camp and lasted for many many days.

CHAPTER XIII
THE TIDE TURNS

THE beginning of October brought about a change of demeanour in the attitude of the Japs towards us. Our rations were cut down considerably and the Japs for a time became more harsh and severe. There were several incidents of face slapping and the temper of the internees was worsening. Our camp representatives appealed to us to grin and bear it, ever reminding us that we were in the power of the Japanese and that there was little we could do about it. Those men whose wives and children were in other camps again began to agitate to be allowed to rejoin them. Colonel Odera then issued a command that the subject was never to be brought up again and that if anybody did so, he would be severely punished. He added that everything possible was being done and that the men must be patient. This for the time being stopped the agitation.

The months dragged on and eventually Christmas came around. We had received the great news of Italy's capitulation and this had raised our hopes, but still Christmas 1943 was a miserable one. We did our best to cheer ourselves up by contributing to the kitchen and having some sort of a Christmas feed and a pudding. What a pudding that was! I don't think anybody knew what went into it, not even the cooks, but we all voted it tops. The beginning of January brought in very cold weather, and as we had no heating whatsoever, many of us felt the cold more than we ordinarily would have done.

Around about March 1944 one more incident occurred, when

the married men again forced our camp representatives to take up the question of rejoining their wives. The ringleader of the movement was Bishop C, a wonderful man and much admired and respected by everybody. He was absolutely fearless and I think I am right in saying that the Japanese too, respected him. However, when our camp representatives interviewed the Colonel regarding this matter, he flew into a terrific rage and shouted and stormed at our representatives. It was a humiliating experience for them. Lieutenant Honda then said that he would address the men. He came over to the Assembly Room and commenced haranguing those present, telling them that it was absolutely forbidden under threat of severe punishment ever to raise the subject again. He reiterated that everything possible regarding this matter was being done and the men must wait for a final decision.

At that Bishop C came forward and said, "May I be permitted to ask a few questions?"

"What do you want?" Honda barked back at him.

At that moment another member of the group called out, "We are with you Bishop in whatever you say." Honda glared around and said, "Who said that?" The man who had spoken came forward and said, "I did."

We then witnessed the spectacle of Honda, who was very short, scrambling up on to the top of the table and fetching our man a resounding slap across his face. Shouts of "bushido" came from every part of the room. "Bushido" supposedly being the spirit of the Japanese nation and the army. Many epithets were hurled at Honda. He scrambled down from the table and looked a bit scared and then turned around and walked out. Later we heard that our representative had asked him why he had struck the man. His reply was, "The man had insulted me." After much argument, it was found that Honda had not even understood what had been said. Later Bishop C was sent for and told that it was known that he was the ringleader, and should a similar occurrence happen again, and should anyone get hurt, he would be shot. We heard that the Bishop replied that man can die but once and that he felt that it was our right to continue to fight against obvious injustices.

Spring came around and with it the great news of the landings in France. We anxiously scanned the newspapers day after day and I must say that the Japanese were very truthful in their account of the progress of the war in Europe. Their news about the Pacific war we could see was

Prisoners at Haiphong Road

absolutely bunkum. They had a commentator whom we called "God's gift to the internees," as we could read between the lines that Japan was getting a hell of a hammering and that the tide had definitely turned in our favour. Many of us kept war maps very openly, until the Japs announced one day that the camp was to be searched. We did not know what they were after, but when they did come around, they collared every map they saw, including maps of Canada. Why, heaven only knows! As soon as the news went around that they were pinching maps, every map very mysteriously disappeared and they did not get many.

They also confiscated any electric appliances we had, such as extra bulbs, wire, immersion heaters, hot plates and so on. They said that there was too much electricity being used, but they never really did manage to get all of our stuff. The Americans in their room had very ingeniously fixed up an electric hot plate in one of the fire places, and the appetising smell of things being fried spread all over the place. Some Jap would smell it and come tearing up the stairs, rush into the room and start in a one man's search. He would find all the men sitting innocently around reading, sewing or writing. He would bellow out, "Where is hot plate?" and everybody would look innocently at him and at each other and ask, "What hot plate?" One American was particularly · brazen in this and would invite the Jap to search the place if he thought that anything was there. The Jap would finally walk out looking very self-conscious and embarrassed. As soon as he had gone down the stairs, the flap in front of the fireplace would be lowered and the cooking would proceed.

The summer of 1944 passed without any untoward incident. The 4th July was celebrated as traditionally as we could possibly celebrate. A grand open air concert was held and the national anthems of all countries represented in the camp were sung quite openly. Old Somekawa, the interpreter, was leaving the camp just as "God Save the King" was being played and he came to a stop in the middle of the roadway and raised his hat. The anthem ended, he replaced his hat and continued on his way out, but had not reached the gate before the "Star Spangled Banner" began to be played. Again, the old chap stopped and again raised his hat. He was not a bad old chap, but of course he was powerless to assist us in any way.

In November 1944, we had our first real air raid. It started off at eight o'clock in the morning and we got our first view of a B-29. It was a magnificent sight and raised the morale of the camp more than I can say. The Japs were throwing everything they had at it, and, much to our glee, nothing came anywhere near that great plane. The Bombers came over in waves until about half past four in the afternoon. Great clouds of smoke hung over the eastern section of the city. Japanese pursuit planes were conspicuous by their absence. We did not let this opportunity go of pulling the Japanese' legs. Some of them got quite annoyed. Ten days later, there was yet another raid and this one proved to be even more thrilling than the previous one. We saw ten great B-29s hurtling through the skies. It was a magnificent sight. Only one Japanese plane rose to contest their progress. It did not stay up for long. The Japanese passed this over lightly in their newspapers and claimed that they had shot down most of the attacking force after it had left the vicinity of the city. Several of our Japanese guards asked us if we believed this, and we said, "What do you think?" and again asked them where their fighters were.

CHAPTER XIV
TRANSPORTED NORTH

O N November 30th we had a grand concert in honour of St. Andrews Day and Winston Churchill's birthday. It was a superb show and proved the old saying, "Necessity was the mother of invention." The scenery produced from nothing was marvellous and the costumes were also excellent. At most of our concerts, many gags were made at the expense of the Japs, but they invariably went right over their heads.

I remember one play we put on, "Journey's End," which brought about rather a funny incident. Those of you who know the play will remember the part where the Captain, trying to conceal his own fear of death, became terribly angry with his fiancee's brother who had joined him. When this part was being rehearsed, Honda happened to be passing the rehearsal room and hearing the shouts within, thought that a fight was taking place. He banged loudly at the door and demanded admittance. When the door was unlocked and opened, be strolled in and asked what all the trouble was about. The producer carefully explained to him that they were rehearsing a play. He asked for the script and ordered them to proceed with the rehearsal. He lost his place half a dozen times and then suddenly made the, to us, exceedingly amusing remark, "Oh yes, I know this play. I studied it in College." With great effort the actors kept their faces straight.

The Japanese have an extraordinarily peculiar sense and idea of celebrations. November 5th being the anniversary of the opening of the camp, they fully expected us to join with them in celebrating the great occasion. They organized a grand concert and asked us to cooperate. Our natural reply was, "What have we to celebrate?" and they said, "But you must. It is a great day." We refused at first, but they retaliated by threatening to prohibit any future concerts or plays if we did not attend. We finally compromised by agreeing to have our band play at the concert and that was the extent of our cooperation.

Room captains, of which I was one, were ordered to attend, properly clothed! It was one of the most boring afternoons that I had ever spent. The dining hall where the concert was held, was packed with Japanese school children and women, who loudly cheered and clapped every item, including the renderings of the camp band. A near-incident occurred at the end, when the Japanese wanted the band to play a patriotic song with Japanese flags all around them. The leader of the band point blank refused, whereupon the bright young Japanese girl who seemed to be running the show threatened to slap him across the face. H, the band leader, said very distinctly, "Miss, if you put your hand on me, I'll hit you so god damn hard, you'll wonder what did hit you." Somekawa, the peace maker, rushed into the breach and prevented any further incident. It was finally agreed that the band would play the patriotic song behind drawn curtains on the stage.

December 1st started the coldest season that Shanghai has ever known. We woke up in the morning to find ice everywhere and the temperature remained below freezing point for 89 days. It is a winter that none of us will ever forget. Most of us were suffering from malnutrition, as the Japanese were only giving us about 1400 calories of food per day. With our own stocks, we raised this to about 1700 or 1800, but this was certainly not enough to keep us warm. Our rooms were absolutely freezing cold and we certainly suffered. No group of people ever looked forward to warm weather more than we did. The only bright spot during that long, hard winter was the arrival of another shipment of Red Cross parcels.

The parcels which arrived were indeed a God-send and all of us will ever be grateful to the Red Cross Societies, principally the American Red Cross Society, for having sent them. The joy of tasting good butter, jam, smoking a real cigarette, it was wonderful. We were supposed to get four parcels each, but the Japanese ordered that only one parcel per month be issued. We felt that there was some ulterior motive behind this order, and this later proved to be only too true. In the meantime, we grumbled and complained, but unfortunately to no avail.

The arrival of the parcels also gave rise to a bitter quarrel between the non-American and American groups. With few exceptions, the best of the Americans had left us in 1943 and those left were indeed a queer mixture. This crowd numbering about 22 claimed all of the American Red Cross parcels to themselves. This would have given each man about 35 parcels! Enquiries made to the International Red Gross Society brought back vague and ambiguous replies. However, the non-American group stood by their guns, maintaining that regardless of nationality we were all in the same boat and it was felt that the American Red Cross would not be making any discrimination, so long as the parcels went to member subjects of the United Nations. Surprisingly the Japs seemed to support this argument. When a parcel issue occurred, the Japs of course, rigorously searched every parcel. What they expected to find I don't know, as every parcel was identical and nothing of a contraband nature was ever discovered. However, the Japanese are a suspicious people, and they were spy mad and trusted nobody. The American Red Cross had also sent quite a considerable quantity of bulk supplies, including overcoats, shoes, underwear, overalls, warm hats and many other things. To these the American group, or I should say the contumacious members of the American group, laid claim, and after many bitter words had been spoken, these were handed over to them. They had far more than they could possibly handle and eventually agreed to hand some of the articles back for distribution among the non-American members. Several of us were so disgusted with their previous behaviour that we were inclined to tell them what they could do with the articles.

What made us feel more bitter was the fact that some of the Greek members, who were exceedingly poor, being ex-seamen, were without warm under clothing or overcoats and here were some of these Americans, or so-called Americans, who had as many as three overcoats. It was also discovered that many of these beautiful American army overcoats were being handed to the Japanese for outside trade for the purpose of obtaining cigarettes and booze. Many, many months afterwards, our original thought that the supplies sent were to be distributed to all members regardless of their nationality was discovered to be absolutely correct, and a notice to this effect appeared on the camp's notice board. I often wondered what these men must have thought.

During the early part of 1945, the Japs had definitely changed, in many ways, in respect to their treatment of us. They were not so tough or strict and we attributed this to the fact that they knew the game was up and that they were trying to get into our good graces. One incident in particular, seemed to bear out this point of view. Three members of the camp, one American and two British had broken into the Japanese store-room early in December 1944 and had stolen a large quantity of cigarettes and had also lifted a considerable amount of sugar. This sugar turned out to be the special sugar blessed by the Emperor and which was to be used in the making of the Japanese New Year rice cakes. None of us knew that this theft had taken place, until one day, the Japanese suddenly descended on us and ordered every man, with the exception of the room captains, out of the room. I, being a room captain, remained behind and saw that they were carefully examining all sugar and cigarettes. Suddenly they all left and the next day, one man, B, was arrested and taken to the Administration Building. Later, the popular American band leader, H, was arrested and later still, D, a Briton, was in turn taken over.

It eventually transpired that these three men had stolen the cigarettes and sugar. Adding insult to injury when they knew that the Japanese were on their track, they had dumped the sacred sugar into the lavatory! We all fully expected to see the little black car come in and see the three culprits disappear — for good. But the days passed by and nothing happened. Shortly after the New Year, the three culprits were sent for and we all thought, here it is, they are going to get it in the neck; but after about half an hour, they came out of the Japanese office grinning broadly, and on being asked what had happened, we found that they had been sentenced to one month's imprisonment!

This imprisonment took the form of having to sit in the guard room from eight o'clock in the morning till eight o'clock at night. They were not supposed to smoke or read, but they did. After having been in durance vile for a few days, it was very laughable to see the three of them going to the guard room every morning well wrapped up against the cold, carrying their easy chairs and a book. B and H during their partial incarceration succeeded in establishing a good arrangement with their guards for future deals in cigarettes and booze. Those two would never let the grass grow under their feet! Many other minor breaches appeared to be overlooked by the Japs and, as I have already said, this gave us the idea that it would not be long before the end came, but much more was to happen before that came about.

During April, vague rumours began to circulate the camp that the Japs had decided to move us to another part of the country. We read in the newspapers that fighting was raging on Okinawa Island and as this Island was only a few hundred miles from Shanghai, we naturally believed that the next point for attack would no doubt be the China coast in general and, of course, Shanghai in particular. This was indeed wishful thinking. In May, Colonel Odera was suddenly transferred. He made a long speech to us thanking us for our good behaviour and telling us how sorry he was to leave us. He asked us to continue with our good behaviour and advised the older men to look after their health during the coming summer months. We thought that we had seen the last of old "handle bars" as we called him but, like a bad penny, he turned up again, but not in Shanghai.

June strengthened the rumour of an imminent departure from Shanghai and this fact was borne out by the Japs withholding the last of the four parcels which should have been distributed in May. They gave no reason for their action. About the middle of June, we were definitely informed that we were to be transported in July. We emphatically protested against this to the Japanese, but their reply was that as Shanghai was likely to become a danger zone, it was their duty to attend to our safety. We replied that we were quite prepared to face the danger and would in no way hold them responsible for anything that might happen to us at the hands of our own Allies, but to no avail, as the Japanese believed us to be dangerous characters and we could not therefore be allowed to stay behind. Needless to say, there were many heavy hearts amongst us, as we did not know at that time where we were going or what awaited us at the other end. Seeing that protesting was of no further use, we started in to prepare for our journey. Though the Japanese began placing double guards around the camp, many messages were slipped out advising our outside friends of our coming departure. The result was that the next parcels day brought a tremendous increase in the number of parcels. There was no celebration of the 4th July, as we were all feeling too fed up and in no way inclined to think of any celebrating.

Impromptu barber, Haiphong Road

We were told to have the bulk of our stuff ready for moving to the Shanghai North Station by dawn July 7th. I was chosen as one of the leaders to go down to the Station. It was the first time I had left Haiphong Road since I had come into the place on January 28th, 1943. It all looked very strange to me and I realized how a man released from gaol must feel when he steps out once more into the open world. Everything seems so big and spacious and the old familiar sights made me feel very nostalgic. The whole of that day we worked like coolies, loading the freight cars. Several friends endeavoured to get near us to have a word or two with us before we left, but the Jap guards saw them off at the trot.

July 8th, the date of departure, I was again sent down to the station to work. Honda had promised the work party that if we finished the job at four o'clock, he would arrange for us to be brought back to the camp for a bath and change of clothes before leaving. As usual, the little swine broke his promise. We worked like galley slaves all day and we had the job completed by half past three. We were all in a filthy state, being absolutely drenched in perspiration and smothered in dust and dirt. Honda turned up at four o'clock and when we asked him where the trucks were to take us back to the camp, he bellowed, "No time, no time. You will march to the station." We emphatically protested and called him every kind of a "son of a bitch" we could lay our tongues to, but he calmly ignored us. We lined-up and started our march to the actual station, which was about a quarter of a mile away. We looked a filthy, bedraggled lot, but being determined to show the thousands of Chinese, who had turned out to look at us that we were not down hearted, we sang the whole way. Many of the Chinese held up their thumbs and cried out "Hao." We vigorously cheered and marched on. The Japanese guards tried to stop us singing, but we took no notice of them and they gave it up as a bad job.

Arriving at the great square in front of the station, we found a vast crowd assembled to watch us go. Amongst them we could see many familiar faces who called out encouraging words to us, telling us to keep our chins up. The place was thick with Japanese military, who kept everybody away from us. We were finally marched on to the platform and herded into the trains. There were many cases where the guards struck the men when they were getting on and two or three near-incidents occurred. Honda was running around like a demented bee shouting and yelling at everybody. We were packed into third class carriages which, dear reader, are a good bit different to a third class carriage in the States or in England.

Hard wood seats and hard wood backs and the backs are straight up and down. An aisle ran up the middle of the carriage, six being seated on one side and four on the other. There were two lavatories per carriage, and these, even before we started, were in a foul and disgusting state. Six guards were assigned to each carriage. We were still standing at the platform at nine o'clock and Honda had told us, the work party, that there was no time for us to go back to have a wash and change! I was feeling absolutely dead tired, aching in every bone and smelt like a horse. At 9.15 we started off.

During the night, despite our weariness, there was no sleep for anybody. We were not allowed to lie on the floor, but had to sit up all the time. Dawn came and found a very tired and bleary eyed lot of men. The whole of the day we kept on going, stopping sometimes for an hour here and there. At the stops the Japanese guards stood at both sides of the train to prevent anyone approaching us. We were too tired and fed up to notice any details of the scenery. We were told that on arrival at Nanking, we would be allowed to have some exercise, but arriving there at half past four, we did not get the promised exercise.

The train was run on to the train ferry for conveyance across the broad Yangtsze to Pukow, the southern terminus of the Pukow/Tientsin Railway. At Pukow we were told that we could get off the train for exercise. It was indeed glorious to be able to stretch our legs and lie down in the sweet smelling grass. Many of the men were already beginning to get swollen feet. No rations had been handed out by the Japs beyond dry rusks and a kind of dog biscuit. We knew that if we wanted to eat, we would have to feed ourselves. The last of the four parcels, which had been issued to us the night before our departure, were indeed a blessing.

Honda seemed determined that we should suffer as much as

possible and he even objected to our being supplied with water. It was only through the kindness of our interpreter, Lance Corporal Endo, that we did manage to get quite a quantity of water to drink and hot water with which to make tea. He was incurring the risk of Honda's displeasure but he seemed to take the chance for us and his assistance to us was something we all deeply appreciated. Everybody spoke well of Endo. We were only allowed the pleasure of twenty minutes exercise at Pukow and were then herded back on to the train. In the meantime, the guards had barb wired all the windows. We learned later that they had done this because the military prisoners from Kiangwan prison camps who had been sent up north two months before had made a break and five of them had managed to make an escape, so they were taking no chances with us.

That night was just as hideous, if not more so than the previous one. No sleep, very sore bottoms and a feeling of absolute exhaustion. Dysentery had broken out amongst us and several men were afflicted. A continuous stream of men were going backwards and forwards to the lavatory. The stench and filth was beyond description. Some of the men had rigged up a device by which they could lean their arms and head in a sort of sling suspended from the luggage rack. One of the men, a Salvation Army officer, was resting in this position when the Jap doctor came around. When the doctor saw him, he got the idea in his head that this man was going to attempt suicide and ordered him to take the contraption down. W asked him why and for reply got a resounding slap across his face. This from a doctor! More Japanese culture!

We arrived at Pengpu early next morning and one of the first men we saw was one of our old sergeant majors who had been in charge of the guards many, many months before. He was a decent old stick named Komatsu. We saw him come out on to the platform yawning and stretching and suddenly his eyes fell on us. His mouth fell open and then he yelled and before you could say "knife" he was across the track reaching up to the windows to shake hands with us. One of the guards leant out and barked something at him and I thought old Komatsu was going to shoot him. He simply barked back at him and the guard, seeing his badges of rank, very rapidly effaced himself. Komatsu came on to the train and expressed absolute amazement on seeing us and saying that he had no idea why we were on our way up north. He told us that he thought that we were heading for a place called Fengtai which was about nine miles from the ancient capital of China, Peking. He said he guessed this because the American military prisoners who had gone through a couple of months ago had been taken there.

He asked us if he could do anything for us and we said we would like some hot water. I don't know who he contacted but the next thing we knew was that Endo was coming down the carriages telling us to get buckets and go with him to collect the necessary hot water. We were all very grateful to old Komatsu for his kindness. I think he was able to do this as Honda had left the train to go and make some arrangements in the town at the military headquarters. About ten o'clock, we started off again and travelled north the whole of that day. By this time, the state of many of the men's feet was very serious. Several of them not only had swollen feet but their feet had burst open and the sores were becoming septic. Our doctor. Doctor S, was working like a Trojan, trying to alleviate the sufferings of the men but the task was entirely beyond him. His staff too did their best for us. One or two of the men who had been suffering from dysentery had become delirious and were moved to the hospital coach, which was just like ours except that there were stretchers strung between luggage racks.

We were then getting into the guerilla country and so travelling at night was out of the question. We spent the night at a wayside station and believe me did those Japs watch us! We were off again at dawn the next morning and began to travel through some really lovely country, but we were all too tired and exhausted to appreciate its beauty. We noticed that every station we passed through was heavily fortified and that along the whole track the Japanese had dug a ditch 10' deep and 15' wide to prevent the guerillas from crossing over and destroying the track. In many places the ditch was filled with water but most of the way along we noticed that it was dry. Evidence that the American fliers had

been busy was apparent as we very often saw locomotives which had been shot up. We were hoping that an attack would be made on our train and thereby give us an opportunity to escape, but no such luck. We heard after the war that strong rumours had got back to Shanghai that

Destroyed train engine, North China

the train had been attacked by guerillas and that we had all been rescued. I wish we had! We arrived at the great city of Tsinan, the capital of the province of Shantung, at about five o'clock that afternoon. After having posted guards all over the place, we were told that we could take exercise on the platform. Fortunately, there was a row of taps with plenty of water in them located right on the platform. A rush was made for these taps in an endeavour to get some of the muck and sweat washed off us, but alas we were only allowed ten short minutes and Honda came rushing on to the platform yelling, "No time, no time. Hurry up get back!" That man was a swine if there was ever one — we spent the whole night at Tsinan.

While at Tsinan we noticed a white man on a train which was lying just across the track from us frantically making signs to us. We were wondering who he was and whilst some of us occupied the attention of the guards, others got into conversation with the stranger. He turned out to be the Swiss Vice Consul of Tientsin and he had been on a visit to another internment camp located at a place called Weihsien. He informed us that he did not think that we would be settling at Fengtai very long as this was only a transition camp. His guess was that we were headed for either Manchuria, Korea or even Japan itself. He had not previously heard that we were on our way up, but promised that he would contact the Swiss Consul at Peking and apprise him of our arrival with the request that he do all he could for us. He told us to keep our chins up as he felt sure that the end was in sight and that it would not be long before we would be on our way south again heading for home. We were hoping that he was right.

CHAPTER XV
FENGTAI AND THE END OF THE WAR

W E started off again very early next morning on what we hoped was the last lap of the dreadful journey, as most of us were by this time absolutely exhausted. I think I had a total of only three hours sleep, and despite the fact that I felt as though I could sleep on a clothes line, I just simply could not get off. We arrived at Tientsin at about three in the afternoon and left that city at about four. North China is notorious for its flies and believe me we had our full share of them. This all went to increasing our misery. A visit to the lavatory was to find it a seething black mass of flies, and it was only when we just could not hold ourselves that we used the place, it was so utterly foul.

We arrived at Fengtai at about half past nine and the first person we saw was none other than old "handle bars" Odera, and the old devil had the audacity to wave to us if he were meeting his long lost brothers. Endo came through and told us that when we got the order to disembark we were to take all our stuff off as we were being marched to the camp, which was "only 1000 meters away." We pointed out to him that many of the men's feet were so badly swollen that it would be absolute torture for them to attempt to walk. We also told him that we had men whose ages ran from 60 to 72 and surely that the Japanese were not so inhuman as to expect them to walk. Endo apologised and said that he could not help it.

We got the order to disembark and after much shouting, shoving, slapping of faces and bangs with the butts of rifles, we were formed into three groups and started off on the march. We learned later that the idea of the march was to show us off to the local populace who had been informed that we were captured American airmen! One look at us by the Chinese gave the lie to the statement and many whispers of "Don't fear" came to our ears, as we passed through those dimly lit streets. We eventually turned up a filthy lane and this appeared to come out to the open country. It was pitch dark and the road along which we were marching had been deeply rutted by car wheels.

We stumbled along, cursing the Japs out loud at every step. Our guards herded us along with shouts of, "hurry up," occasionally using their rifle butts. The distance we walked was actually over a mile and a half. The group that I was in point blank refused to go any further until we had a rest, and our guards re-

Fengtai Prison Camp

alizing that we had just about got to the end of our tether, allowed us to sit down for ten minutes and have a smoke; that is to say those who had a cigarette smoked. After the rest we carried on and finally passed through a big gateway. In the distance, about a quarter of a mile away from us, we could see a great glare of arc lights gleaming and we reckoned that this was the camp. It was.

I remember now that cold feeling that went over me when I first saw the building we were going into and the barbed wire fence that surrounded it. We noticed that the barbed wire was attached to insulators which indicated that it was electrified. We passed through the gates of the enclosure in which our building stood. It turned out to be a huge godown or warehouse with windows very high up on the wall. The floor was made of brick and hard dirt. Each group was assigned to certain sections of the godown. We were told to dump our stuff and reassemble immediately.

When we reassembled, a proclamation was read to us which half of us were too tired to listen to, let alone understand. We learned later that it was a warning that we would be shot for this, shot for that and shot for the other. We were too exhausted to care what we were to be shot for. The Japs then issued us with a bowl of some sort of hot soup each. I don't know what it was, but it was certainly appreciated. As soon as we had this, we moved to our various sections and when I got to my allotted place, I just sank to the brick floor and passed completely out.

I was so exhausted that the four and a half hours I had slept was not nearly sufficient, and I had to be literally kicked before I could get my eyes open and stay awake. We turned up for roll call and as soon as that was over, I went straight back to my brick floor, forgot all about breakfast, and went sound off to sleep again. I think 75% of the men in camp did likewise. I woke up again at 12 o'clock feeling very much better. We had our mid-day meal and were then informed that we would have to unload the baggage vans. We were expecting to have to go back to Fengtai railway station to effect the unloading, but to our utter surprise, we found that they had brought the loaded freight wagons right into a siding inside the walls of the camp. In other words, the march from the station the night before had absolutely been unnecessary. It was just another form of torture on the part of the Japanese.

Fengtai camp was in reality a huge railway depot. It contained over 37 very large godowns or warehouses. There was plenty of space in between the many godowns and scattered around in these spaces were large dumps of material. It was so huge that it was not until the war was nearly over that we discovered that there was a prison camp in another corner containing 2000 Chinese prisoners of war. Our particular camp was a huge building divided into five sections, shaped like an aeroplane or airship hangar and surrounded by barbed wire. The barbed wire was fitted so that it could at any moment be electrified, but this the Japanese never did.

There were no washing arrangements and there were no facilities for lavatories or latrines. Our first job was to dig a deep trench and lay two planks over them for use as latrines. The Japanese supplied us with no disinfectants, so that in no time the files multiplied by the millions. It was particularly hard on the older members of the camp to have to use latrines of this kind, but appeals to the Japs brought no relief to this intolerable situation. They merely said you must fix up something yourselves. The only good things about the place were good air and good water. The water supply was from an Artesian well situated outside our enclosure.

When anybody wanted to draw water, he took his bucket along with him, then had to halt in front of the guard room, which was inside the enclosure, put his bucket down, take his hat off and bow to the sentry. He then proceeded out of the enclosure to the Artesian well and got his water. The same procedure of bowing had to be observed on his return. There was no double roofing to the godown and, in consequence thereof, the heat became absolutely unbearable by noon. Most of the doors leading into the godown sections were shut at night and the temperature at midnight was very often 98°F. The kitchen for the camp was situated near the main gate which was about a quarter of a mile from our enclosure. Food had to be brought from the kitchen on trolleys. The Japs provided very little or no meat, as a matter of fact we only obtained 360 lbs of what was alleged to be camel meat from them in the six weeks that we were there. Vegetables were also hard to get and we practically lived on beans, beans and more beans and a certain amount of millet.

During the unloading of the freight wagons, one of my pals Reggie and I made a discovery. We were carrying a couple of crates which we discovered to contain beer! Right under the very nose of the sentry who had been placed there to guard us, we managed to snaffle two bottles. Though it was Japanese beer, it tasted simply marvellous. Before replacing the empties, we carefully cracked them and replaced the crown corks. It took us two days to unload the freight vans but we did not mind as it gave us something to do. We were not permitted to play any games whatsoever, and our only exercise consisted of walking up and down the space between the building and the barbed wire. "There was a big fire tank which was about 20' in diameter and 10' deep which we started in using as a swimming pool, but the Japs, who could not bear to see us enjoy ourselves in any way, very soon put a stop to this recreation.

Prisoners in front of the warehouses of the Fengtai camp

About two weeks after we had been at Fengtai, we could see that the Japs were very uncertain as to what they were going to do with us. Were they going to move us or were they going to keep us there for duration? In true Jap fashion they could not make up their minds. They kept on moving us from one section of the godown to another — as they stated, they were about to prepare proper cubicles for us to house us during the winter months. Nothing, however, happened and after a week, it always fell on a Sunday, they would move us back to the section they had moved us from the previous Sunday.

About the end of July, we saw three very thin, dirty and bedraggled white men being brought in escorted by gendarmes and soldiers. They were taken to the Japanese Administration quarter which was on the opposite side of the road from our place, and after about an hour, they were put in with us. They turned out to be three Italians, who had been arrested about six weeks before. For what, they did not know. They discovered later that it was the Japanese plan to shoot all three, but they owed their lives to the intervention of a Catholic priest, who, somehow or the other, discovered the plot and threatened to report it to the Vatican. The Japs therefore promised to intern them with us. They told us that Italy had declared war on Germany and also Japan! They also told us that in their opinion, Japan was on her last legs and that the war would soon be over. We, of course, had heard stories like this before, and laughed at them. They were quite decent fellows and soon became quite popular members of our community.

A week after that, we saw three more men being brought in, tied up with ropes and handcuffed. One man we could see, could hardly walk, as he was so emaciated. They were also taken over to the Japanese quarter, allowed to have a bath and change into clothes sent over to them by us. They were then brought over and put into the end section of our godown, which was wired off. Their section adjoined one of ours and it did not take our boys long to dig a hole under the door separating the two sections and enter into conversation with them. They turned out to be three American fliers who had been shot down over various parts of China and brought to our camp after varying periods of incarceration in many different places. One of the men was in a very bad state of emaciation, having been In Japanese hands for some time. The other two were not in such bad shape. We were strictly forbidden to have any conversation with them whatsoever, but of course, that difficulty was very easily overcome.

All this time Honda was becoming more obnoxious than ever and did his best to make life as unbearable as possible for us. He ordered that the doors between sections be closed. This, of course, cut off whatever draft there was and the temperature inside the building rose considerably. He would never give the order himself but in his own shifty way, would deputise Endo, the interpreter, to do his dirty work for him. He continued to pay his daily visits to us and many of the men would ask him when he thought the war would end. His reply was as follows: "Never. The Japanese will never be beaten. They will fight until they win. The Japanese cannot lose."

When he was asked why we could not play baseball and thereby relieve the monotony of the life in camp, he would give one of his two stock replies which were "I don't know" and "I will consider."

About the 9th August, the Japanese suddenly brought a large number of Chinese carpenters into the place and started in constructing the cubicles for us. They had guards all over the place, to try and prevent any conversation between the Chinese and us. However, we had many Chinese speaking people with us and by various means, it was discovered on the 11th August that Russia had joined in the war and was sweeping through Manchuria. This naturally raised our morale. On the night of the 12th August, we heard a terrific uproar going on over in the Japanese quarters. There was much shouting and argument and this went on till the small hours of the morning. Next day the 13th, the

Manual labour in the Fengtai camp

guards who had been stationed inside the enclosure were suddenly withdrawn and we noticed the Japs busily carrying arms from the Formosan quarters to their own. This greatly mystified us and we wondered what it was all about.

A few venturesome spirits then opened the gate at the east end of our enclosure and took a short excursion into the open space, which was the Japanese ball ground. Nobody said anything, so they increased the distance of their walks and within an hour practically the whole camp was walking up and down the baseball field. Some more venturesome than the rest, went on an exploring expedition and it was then that they discovered the Chinese prisoners of war in the other part of the great compound. We could see the guards still standing around the perimeter wall, but they in no way interfered with the explorers. Some of us went up as far as the kitchen and saw some Jap soldiers in a sort of blacksmith shop. We were amazed to see that they were making spear heads. They informed us that they were going to use these to fight the Americans with if they came to Fengtai! We were back to medieval times!

At four o'clock in the afternoon, Honda appeared on the scene and nearly went mad when he saw us wandering around outside the enclosure. He screamed and yelled at us and literally frothed at the mouth while he was driving us back into the enclosure. It was a remarkable sight! We discovered after the war that the reason for these peculiar happenings was that the news of the atomic bombing of Japan had reached the Japanese guards in the camp. There were two factions, a fanatical crowd led by a man we knew as "Hair-lipped Harry" and another and more rational faction led by Endo. The fanatics were in favour of throwing gasoline on our building, setting light to it and as we ran out, shooting us down.

The rational crowd, however, was against this as they pointed out to the fanatical crowd that there were now 360 of us and only about 18 or 20 real Japanese, so that if we burst out and overwhelmed them, there would be hell to pay, as we were a desperate lot and had no doubt armed ourselves with many different kinds of weapons. The two factions finally compromised by the idea of appealing to the 200 Formosans, which were stationed in the camp as guards, to join them. If the Formosans agreed, then the plot was to be carried out, if not, it was to be abandoned. Thank God the Formosans, knowing that the war was nearly over, decided against the idea, hence the removal of all the Formosans' rifles the next day. The Japanese, notoriously one-track minded and being very worried about the situation, forgot all about us and therefore we got away with the running around the main camp confines.

On the night of the 15th of August, one of our Japanese speaking members who was quite friendly with one of the Formosan guards got the astounding news from him that "Japanese American have shake hands. War finished." Mish told the Formosan not to pull his leg, but the soldier assured him that it was true. Mish hurried back to us to impart the exciting news but we had heard so many rumours of this nature that we gave him the bronx cheer. There was a Japanese medical orderly whom we nicknamed "The Nightingale" and who was quite a decent chap and whom we persuaded to come over from the hospital to talk to us. We got him into the corner and asked him if the news was true. He first of all said, "I don't know," but on being pressed, he said, "Very sorry, I cannot speak." We patted him on the back and let him go. That was all we wanted to know, but we were still very sceptical about it all. There was very little sleep that night in camp as everybody was too excited. There was a constant stream of men walking from the building to the latrines and back again.

Next morning, the reveille was sounded as usual and we saw the Japanese and Formosans line up to do their usual kowtow to the Emperor, after which they came over and we had the usual roll call. There was no sign of any end to the war. At ten o'clock in the morning, however, Endo came over and as I was near the gate, he asked me where the two camp representatives were. I conducted him to the Office and with my ears flapping heard him say, "The Colonel and Lieutenant Honda request that you please come over to their office."

C and W left our enclosure and their progress to the Japanese office was watched by everybody. We saw them go in and do the usual bow to the Colonel and Honda. Then we saw them invited to take seats! They were over there for about half an hour and when they finally rose, we noticed that they had dispensed with the usual bow. Endo preceded them out and we saw him engage them in earnest conversation for a few minutes. They then walked towards us, raised their arms with thumbs up. We knew then that it was over! We were still alive! There was no cheering. Everybody just turned around and looked at each other. We were too overcome to demonstrate in any way other than to shake hands with each other and say "Thank God."

A Captains' meeting was immediately called and the official announcement was made that a sort of a truce had been arranged

between Japan and the other countries and that Endo had particularly asked our representatives to request the men not to in any way mock Japanese soldiers. I must say that we respected this request. A committee was immediately formed and this committee fully empowered to represent us, went over to the Japs and made demands for more food, cigarettes, soap and many other things and also complete freedom to wander about the camp. They also de-

The author after the end of the war was announced

manded that in order to avoid any untoward incidents, that all the guards were to be withdrawn from the vicinity of our enclosure. We also asked for a radio. We further demanded the immediate release of the three American fliers. All these demands, with the exception of more food, which the Japanese said was very hard to get, were agreed to. We gave the American fliers a great welcome to our midst. The Japs provided us with three radios, all of which were broken, but our experts very soon put one of them in order and we were soon listening to news from the outside world. It was great news indeed.

On the 17th of August, we heard a droning noise in the skies which turned out to be a B-29 flying very low towards Peking. We saw it circle the Peking Western Air Field a few times and then we saw seven parachutes open up, after which thirty-eight more were dropped. Our American Air Force friends were standing there with us and explained that the first seven we had seen were men and the remainder were supplies. The plane, after dropping its load, circled the field a few more times and then came towards our camp. We rushed out on to the ball ground and frantically waved our arms, shirts, towels, indeed anything we could get to wave to attract their attention. They spotted us all right as the plane changed course and flew down low over the camp and gave us the victory waggle with their wings. We were wildly excited at the sight of the B-29 and we were all feeling that our early release was near at hand. However, the day passed and to us impatient prisoners, the time passed very slowly and we began to imagine that our existence in Fengtai was unknown to our people.

On the same day, we made a demand to the Japanese that all the articles which they had confiscated from us from time to time be returned. What followed again illustrates the unpredictable-ness of the Jap, To our absolute and utter astonishment, practically every article which they had confiscated from us during our years of imprisonment were returned, such as home made immersion heaters, home made frying pans and more valuable articles such as electric razors, maps, hot plates and my beloved camera, projector, used film and 500' of unused film, When we left Shanghai, I had said goodbye to my equipment, but here was

another promise which had been kept by the unpredictable Jap, It was indeed amazing. Needless to say, I very soon got my camera loaded and commenced taking pictures right and left. I even managed to get "old handle bars," the Colonel, to pose and the picture that

Soup time at the Fengtai camp

he permitted me to take, proved to be to a great extent his un-doing two years later, when he was being tried before the War Crimes Court, but more about this later.

The 18th of August came and we still had not heard from either the American Rescue Team which we had seen being dropped by parachute or from the Swiss Consul, but at about half past five on the evening of the 18th, we were notified by the Japs that we would be joined by some more Americans who were coming from Peking. We were warned that it would be wise to save them some food, as they were likely to be hungry. As usual, the Japs would not tell us who they were. At ten o'lock that night we saw a procession of cars coming into the camp and we all crowded out to see who the new arrivals were.

They turned out to be none other than Commander Cunningham of Wake Island fame, accompanied by six men who sometime before had accomplished the almost-impossible, that was, actually escaping from the escape proof Ward Road Gaol in Shanghai. They had made the break at the same time as Commander Woolley of the British Navy, Commander Smith of the American Navy and another service man named Storey. These three, who had plotted the break with a convict who had been released, managed to make a clean get away, but Cunningham and his men were spotted, betrayed and recaptured. They looked a pitiful sight when they arrived. Some of them were terribly thin and others looked fat, but that was caused through the puffiness of Beri Beri. They had been subjected to terrible tortures by the Japs during their Imprisonment in Nanking.

The Japs had originally sentenced them to death on the ridiculous charge of desertion from his Imperial Japanese Majesty's Armed Forces! Their sentence, however, was eventually commuted to life imprisonment, While at Nanking, some of them had been subjected to the raw hide straight jacket treatment, which consisted of being bound tightly in a raw hide straight jacket, having a bucket of water poured over them and then placed in the sun. The results can be well imagined. One man was still suffering from a broken rib. They had not done this to Cunningham, as he was suffering badly from dysentery at the time and they expected him to die anyway.

As the threat of invasion and possible capture by the American Forces of Nanking loomed, the Japs decided to move these dangerous characters to Peking. At half past seven on the evening of the 18th August, they had suddenly been taken out of their cells and lined up and told to wait. They were wondering what this meant. Were they due for another shift or were they due to face the firing squad? After waiting about half an hour, a Japanese officer appeared accompanied by an interpreter. He read something to them in Japanese and when he had concluded his speech, the Japanese interpreter briefly stated, "Gentlemen, the war is over." He continued, "You are now going to be transferred to a place where you will join your fellow countrymen. We trust that you will forget the unpleasant things that have happened in the past. We are sorry about this. To you. Commander Cunningham, we express our apologies, as you, as an officer, should have received better treatment."

Can you imagine the absolute gall of this speaker? After having nearly killed them with ill-treatment and torture, he was now asking them to kiss and make up.

Whilst they had been in the Peking prison, they had learned by various means of the existence of three of the Doolittle fliers, who had been captured in 1942. Commander Cunningham asked the interpreter where the fliers were and demanded their release. The interpreter looked at him with a blank look and exclaimed that he did not know what he was talking about, as there were no Doolittle fliers or any other Americans in the prison. This was later proved to be an absolute lie. We gave the boys a great welcome and fed them as royally as we possibly could. They had not tasted food like that for years. Our doctor requested us to leave them alone so that they could get some sleep and a peaceful rest, but they said to him, "Doctor, we have not been able to talk for a long time. We have got a lot to say and we like to hear the sound of our own voices and the voices of our fellow men. For God's sake, don't chase the boys away. Let us talk ourselves out." The doctor understandingly walked away.

August 19th was a Sunday and it was decided to hold a Thanksgiving Service. Our camp band got out its motley assembly of instruments, many of which were home made, and industriously practised the hymns which were to be sung at the service. The affair was a complete success and was attended by every member. We were well supplied with clergy, as we had with us two Bishops, another Reverend gentleman and two members of the Salvation Army. Believe me, we put our backs into the singing and the national anthems which we sang might have been heard in Peking, nine miles away. The Japs were conspicuous by their absence during this celebration.

Just after the service, the camp representatives and our special committee were summoned to the office by Colonel Odera who, with a broad smile on his face, told them that the camp was closing that night and he requested us to have all our traps packed up to be ready to move to Peking by half past four. On arrival at Peking, we were to be installed in two very nice Japanese Hotels. To the Colonel's absolute astonishment, one of the members of the committee rose and said, "Colonel, we are not

Prisoners swimming in the forbidden fire tank

going! Do not think for one moment you are going to get away with it as easily as that. We are not moving from here until the American representatives of the Army come here and see the foul conditions under which you have been keeping us. We want them to see those packed rooms, the filthy latrines, the maggots, the flies, the food we have been getting, in short, everything."

"But you don't understand," the Colonel said. "We are taking you to two very nice hotels where you will receive good food which will help to build you up." Our representative replied that the nice hotels and good food could wait, whereupon the Colonel after further attempts to be nice, finally lost his temper and banged on the table with his fist, and for the last time showed up as a true Jap, shouting out, "You will go to Peking as I have ordered. Remember I still have the guns!" Our representative then said,"In the face of a show of force like this, we have no alternative than to go, but we do so under protest."

Later it was revealed that Odera had been ordered by the American Rescue Team to produce us in Peking by mid-day August 20th, but he had refrained from telling us this, as it would have meant a complete loss of "face" for him to show us that he was taking orders from an American. Had he told us this in the first place, we would have obeyed without hesitation.

We immediately set to work packing up our things getting ready to move and by half past four in the afternoon were all ready, but when the hour arrived, there was no sign of any trucks. The hours passed and by half past seven we still saw no sign of transport. By this time getting very impatient, we were foraging around among Japanese stores and there found to our great delight large quantities of saki, the national Japanese drink, and

Jubilant prisoners leaving Fengtai

beer. Needless to say, we grabbed the lot and most of the members of the camp became quite tight in a very short while after the discovery of this treasure trove. The trucks finally arrived at half past nine or ten. We chalked Union Jacks, Stars and Stripes and many other flags on to the sides of the trucks. Our Jap guards who were to accompany us kept rubbing them out, but as fast as they rubbed, we put them back again, so that they finally gave it up as a bad job.

We started off on the nine mile road to Peking, all feeling exceedingly pleased with ourselves and singing. During the ride through the country, we never saw a soul, the whole countryside being in complete and absolute darkness, but as we passed through the gates in the outer wall of Peking, we saw a few Chi-

nese who immediately started to clap and cheer us. The
further we got into Peking,
the more people were gathered on the pavements and
the louder became the cheering and clapping.

Just before we entered
the Tartar city, our con-
voy had to stop to allow

*Japanese or Formosan soldiers leaving Feng-
tai at the conclusion of the war*

a train to pass by. Here there were simply thousands of Chinese and the welcome they gave us was simply stupendous.
They could see that we were not troops, but nevertheless it was
a sign to them that Peking's travail was over and the heel of the
Japs had been removed. They threw us fruit and cigarettes, and
they ran up to the sides of the trucks to shake hands with us.
Many of us were completely overcome by the welcome they
gave us. Our guards directly withdrew to the centre of the truck
and sat down well out of sight. Many of them had handed their
rifles over to their former prisoners and these rifles were waved
wildly in the air. The rest of the journey to the hotel was indeed a
triumphal trip. Cheers, laughter, smiles, greeted us everywhere.

On arrival at the hotel, which we learned later had been con-
structed to contain a Japanese geisha house, or more broadly
speaking, a Japanese brothel which was due to have been opened
on August 15th, we had a near incident. A Sergeant Major whom
we had nicknamed "Clark Gable" was standing waiting for us.
The Japanese custom on entering a house, as many of you probably know, is to remove your shoes. This, of course, never entered
our heads. We just piled in with our dirty boots. "Clark Gable"
was standing at the head of the short flight of steps leading from
the patio into the reception hall.

In his old style, he shouted out, "Stop, take away shoes." He
was immediately greeted with cat calls and yells of, "Get the hell
out of it," and a rush was made at him. Endo, however, dashed

through the crowd and pushed the Sergeant Major to one side and turning around appealed to us to take off our shoes before we entered the rooms which we were to occupy, as there was new tatami on the floors, and for our own sakes, it would be better to keep these clean. We told him, "O.K. Endo, but we advise you to get that bastard out of the way before we kill him." Endo promised to have this matter attended to.

Of course, there was little or no sleep for any of us that night. We were too busy and too excited talking, drinking the remains of the stolen saki and beer and eating. We just couldn't seem to get enough to eat. The next morning we received a request through our representatives from the American Rescue Team that we remain in our quarters and not attempt to go out, as the city was full of Japanese soldiery and it was their aim to avoid any untoward incidents of any kind. They promised us that as soon as the situation had settled a bit that we could do as we pleased. We respected this request.

At one o'clock that day, the Rescue Team led by Major Nichols appeared on the scene, with them were Odera and Honda, They proceeded to the reception office of the hotel and our representatives requested us to retire, so that the meeting could be proceeded with. Major Nichols, however, said, "Don't chase them away, when they have been waiting for this for a long time. Stick around boys and enjoy yourselves." He then pointed his finger at Honda and said, "What are you going to do about feeding these men?" For the last time Honda came across with his old answer "I don't know."

Nichols levelled his finger at him and said, "Don't you tell me that and don't you use that expression to me again. Your commanding officer in this area has informed me that if you small boys do not do as you are told, he is going to use the big stick on you and I will see that he does."

We were tickled to bits to see the great Honda so humiliated. He richly deserved it. His reply to this was, "I will immediately see about it."

"You had god damn well better!" Nichols said.

He then turned to Odera and said to him, "I want the three Doolittle fliers." Odera looked at him with a blank look on his face and said that he did not know anything about them. Nichols then made an astounding statement: "You are a damn liar, Odera. I know that you saw these men last Tuesday at half past five and I want them." Odera was dumb-founded on hearing this and immediately promised to look into the matter. Nichols told him to get on to it right away. In the meantime, the other members of the Rescue Team had been telling us about the Atomic Bomb, but our minds just could not grasp the stupendousness of it all. One aptly described it as being like a scene from a page in H.G. Wells' *The Shape of Things to Come*. We then realized why the Japs at Fengtai had wanted to kill us all.

The Team, Odera and Honda then departed and I got an excellent picture of Odera looking very worried as he left. We heard later that he had appeared at the Hotel de Pekin at about half past five that evening with two of the Doolittle boys, who were in a very bad state of emaciation, resulting from the terrible treatment that they had received. Odera, on being asked where the third man was, replied that he was dead. Nichols then ordered him to produce the body or ashes of the man and also his personal effects. Odera departed looking very worried.

He turned up again about an hour later saying that he had the body of the flier in his car. Nichols summoning our doctor, immediately went out and saw a pitiful body lying in the bottom of the car, apparently dead. He was carried up to the hospital, which was located in the Hotel, and we heard that though he was to all appearances dead, Dr. S went to work on him and pulled off an absolute miracle. He resuscitated the poor fellow and after a terrific battle which lasted over three days, brought him back to life and sanity. His suffering during his imprisonment must have been indescribable.

CHAPTER XVI
THE JOURNEY HOME

WE spent a very pleasant month in Peking where we were most kindly treated by the populace of that great city. Every door was opened to us and the kindnesses shown was something that none of us will ever forget. Many of us had an opportunity which would not come to us again—of seeing a really historical city at no cost. None of us had any money and we did not feel like asking any of our many benefactors to help us out. That was one of the reasons, I think, why many of us were anxious to return to our homes as we did not like the idea of living on charity. Of course, naturally, the main reason for wanting to get back was to rejoin our families again.

Some of the more fortunate ones had already been flown back to Shanghai or directly to their homelands, but the majority could not be thus accommodated and we just had to kick our heels around and wait. This made us more and more impatient and I am afraid that our kindly American rescuers must have got a very bad opinion of us from the way we were continually pressing them on the question of returning. They patiently explained to us that it would be quite a job to get 350 men and their effects back to Shanghai and this job would require some planning. They told us that the return by rail was impossible as from information received, they had heard that the railway system had been completely disrupted.

About this time, I met a Chinese friend of mine who informed me that he was going to try the journey by rail. He said that he had heard that the railway had been more or less repaired, but that the journey would take about five days (normally the trip takes 39 hours only). I pointed out to him that I was completely without funds, but he generously replied that he would look after me in that respect and that I had no need to worry. I approached Colonel Ramp who was in charge of us, and informed him of my intentions. He told me that as I was a free man, he could not in any way prevent me from going, but warned me that whatever I did was entirely on my own responsibility, but that for his part, he would be glad to render me any assistance he possibly could. I asked him to supply me with some food and he very kindly instructed his quartermaster to let me have rations for five days. Before going on with my story, I would like

The author (2nd right) with friends in Peking

to record my deep appreciation for the many kindnesses shown to us by the American Forces, who came to our rescue. Nothing seemed to be too much trouble for them and they were indeed, the personification of patience and kindness.

I left Peking for Tientsin on September 22nd where I was met by my Chinese friend, Mr. Chen. We spent the day looking the city over. I had been there before but was only seven years old when I had last seen the place. Chen told me that he had got tickets for as far as Tsinan, a big city south of the Hoang Ho — the Yellow River — in Shantung, and that we were due to leave early next morning. We got to the station at 5.30 a.m. on September 23rd, where we found a huge crowd assembled at the entrance to the platform. We pushed through and after talking nicely to the ticket collector got on the train before the mob got going. When the gates were opened, there was a mad scramble for places and the overflow determined not to be left behind, piled onto the roofs of the carriages and over the front of the engine.

Finally at 7.15, we started off, heading south. I can't describe my feelings. At last I was really free and headed for Home. Its a grand word that—Home! At times we rolled along at a fairly good clip—about 25 miles per hour, but at other times when passing over sections of the rails which had been destroyed and repaired, the speed dropped to about 2 miles an hour and the train rocked slowly from side to side. Smashed carriages and overturned locomotives became a familiar sight. For miles you wouldn't see a whole telegraph pole, all of them having been carefully sawn through and the insulators smashed.

Fortunately for the roof riders there were no tunnels, but the proceedings were frequently enlivened by a yell and we would look out in time to see one of the roof riders rolling down the embankment having probably fallen asleep and rolled off the roof. Of course, the train never stopped and the poor devil was left to fare as best he could in the middle of nowhere looking very dazed, fed up and far from home. If his fellow roof riders felt kindly disposed towards the victim, they would throw his few belongings off the train. If not, it was just too bad. Incidentally, the more fortunate "inside riders" who witnessed these tumbles would be greatly amused and laugh like hell, passing the incident off with the expression, "Muh yu fa dze," which roughly translated means, "Too bad it was so fated to happen."

We arrived at a place called Tehchow in the evening, where I met some friends who were on their way north and told me that they had been nearly five weeks on the road. They told a story of destroyed tracks, burning bridges and frequent brushes between the 8th Route Army and the Jap train guards—my friends' goods wagon being hitched onto a military train. It didn't sound too promising but Chen and I were determined to push on. We had to spend the night at Tehchow, it being, we were informed, too dangerous to travel by night. So we made ourselves as comfortable as possible and spent a troubled night being eaten alive by mosquitoes and hearing sounds of distant shooting and explosions.

However, next morning we started off again and after an uneventful day we arrived at Tsinan at 3.30 p.m. We managed to find lodgings for the night in the only European hotel in Tsinan, which was owned by a German. There we met an American Flying Officer who had been shot down not far from Tsinan some two months before and had been wandering around all this time dodging the Japs on one side and bandits on the other. He didn't even know the war was over until a few days before our arrival, when, having heard the good news, he made his way into Tsinan where he was joined by a member of the Chinese American Forces who had been flown to Tsinan to render assistance.

As can well be imagined, we had a good night together and the proceedings were enlivened by the German hotel owner's wife pulling off the "happy event act." We all assisted in rushing the good Frau off to the hospital but I never did get to know whether it was a boy or a girl or both, because we were off early next morning. With the help of our new friend, George Hwa, of the Chinese American Forces, we managed to get seats for the next stage which we thought was going to take us right through to Hsuchowfu. We travelled through the usual scenes of destruction, ruined and burnt out station buildings, burnt out guard towers which the Japanese had so painstakingly erected for the defence of the railway, and the wreckage of passenger cars, freight cars and locomotives.

We arrived at Yenchowfu some time after 9.00 p.m. and again settled down for the night on the train. Early next morning we were awakened and told to hurry up and get off the train which was returning in half an hour to Tsinan. We asked, "What about going on to Hsuchowfu?" and were told that the rail ended there and how we were going to get to Hsuchowfu they did not know, so we piled out. Much to my surprise, I ran into a group of people, Europeans, whom I had not seen for nearly four years. After the greetings they gave me the cheering news that they had been at Yenchowfu for a week with no immediate prospect of going on further for some time to come! Enquiries revealed that a Jap military repair train left for the South every day and returned at night.

So after breakfast, which was eaten in a Chinese street restaurant, we repaired to the local Jap military headquarters and interviewed numerous Jap officers whom I informed that I was a returning P.O.W. and that by the terms of the peace, they were bound to assist me to get home. This worried them a bit, but after much argument, they agreed to let our party have the use of a freight wagon attached to the repair train leaving next day.

That night Chen and I slept at the German Catholic Mission where the Fathers were most kind and hospitable. After a good breakfast next morning, we got down to the station and loaded our party, which numbered about 40, including several women and two children, onto the freight wagon. We had a terrific job fighting off the huge mobs of refugees who were trying to swarm on. At 9.30 a.m. we started off. I must describe here what a military repair train looks like. The motley assortment of rolling stock was headed by three empty freight cars, then comes the engine and then a long string of freight wagons loaded with materials, troops and plastered with refugees. About 200 yards behind, another locomotive followed us to pull us out if we got into trouble. In the leading empty car, a man stands with a green and red flag and his job is to keep his eye on the track and so long as everything is all right, he waves his green flag, but if he spots anything wrong, up goes the red flag.

We went buzzing along at the high speed of 5 m.p.h. for two hours with Johnny in the car merrily waving his green flag, when suddenly up went the red and we came to a sudden and very noisy stop. We piled out and went along to see what was wrong and discovered that the rails had been disconnected and the bolts, nuts and spikes missing. The Japs said the missing parts would probably be in the fields so we started a search and, sure enough, found most of the missing parts. We gave the Japs a hand to repair the track, after which, we nervously stood by whilst the train passed over the repaired section and then jumped on. We had not been going ten minutes when, after rounding a bend, we again came to another shuddering stop. This time, we found that the 8th Route Army Boys, whom the Chinese call "Ba Loo

Jen," had really made a tip-top job of railway wrecking. The track for about 200 yards had been removed, the embankment dug away and the sleepers piled up and set on fire. They were still burning when we arrived on the scene. We could see that it would take at least

Wrecked line on the journey to Shanghai

two days to effect repairs so we decided to walk to the next station which was about three miles away and was called Chosien. We managed to hire some farmer boys to carry our stuff which they agreed to do — for a price. We eventually arrived at Chosien which we found to be a small sized town.

From enquiries made, we found that there might be trains leaving from a place called Liang Hsiao Tien which was about 35 miles further down the line. There was nothing else for it, but to walk. All the men of the party got together and after a conference held in a Chinese street restaurant, it was decided to chance the walk.

We got hold of the owner of a wheel barrow and arranged with him to bring all his colleagues along, which he did, and after a wallah wallah which lasted for two hours, a bargain was struck and we engaged about 40 wheel barrows for the trek to Liang Hsiao Tien. The wheel barrows used are very big, being an outsize in this type of vehicle. It is managed by two men, one fore and one aft, and they are assisted occasionally by a donkey which is hitched by traces to the barrow. I say occasionally, because the donkey just trots in front with the traces slack and every now and then, the leading barrow man yells at the animal and flicks it with a whip. This stirs the donkey to life and for a matter of 50 yards or so, the donkey really puts in some hard work and then it slacks off again, until the next yell and flick of the whip. The barrows can carry six to eight people and luggage.

To ensure a full parade next morning, we insisted that the wheel barrow men assemble their barrows and donkeys in the compound of the caravanserai that night which they finally agreed to do. Later we wished we hadn't, as the night was made hideous by the constant braying of the donkeys. Sleep came in snatches as we lay on the hard kangs or sleeping dais inside the one story building allotted to us. Mosquitoes and bed bugs also made the night interesting. Dawn was indeed most welcomed.

After breakfast we assembled the caravan and were joined by some Chinese families of the better class who had travelled down with us from Tientsin. They wanted to get in with us for safety as we were due to pass through the worst of the bandit and Ba Loo Jen country. We spaced them out amongst us and after much shouting by the coolies and the braying of donkeys, we got underway.

Chen and I led the way. We had instructed the barrow men that they must keep as near to the railway as possible. However, after going for about half an hour, I noticed that they were heading away from the line and keeping to a sort of main road, Questioning our men, we were told that we would soon be turning in again. Shortly after this, we were approaching a village when we were suddenly stopped by armed men who told us that we couldn't go this way, as there were Ba Loos on the other side of the village who had held up a caravan the day before and after having robbed it, they had kidnapped six people.

I was not prepared for what happened next. Chen, who stands about 5' 3" and was by no means muscular, walked up to our leading barrow man and calmly socked him and then in no uncertain way proceeded to lay the law down. I fully expected a scrap, but to my amazement, the barrow coolie took it like a lamb and looked very sheepish. Incidentally, the barrow coolie was a six footer and beautifully built. He explained that by taking the main road through the country a few miles could be saved. Chen told him that the saving of miles didn't matter, but the saving of lives did, so hurry up and about turn to the railway line.

To turn a caravan round on a narrow country road is a feat. With much yelling, cursing and in clouds of dust the feat was accomplished and in due course, we arrived back at the line. The track beside the line was the worst imaginable, it being only 18" wide and at frequent intervals it was broken by deep ditches. This is where the donkeys came in. With yells of "Dree! Dree!" and the liberal application of the whip, the barrows were pushed down one bank and up the other in a jiffy. Its marvellous how those barrow men kept their vehicles balanced and on an even keel. Out of over 40 barrows only one was overturned during the 35 mile trek!

We frequently had to cross rivers which fortunately were nearly dry or shallow. Even then we had to wade knee or waist deep. One good thing about wading was that it certainly refreshed us. The country we passed through was very lovely. Vast plains all under cultivation and ranges of hills and mountains in the distances. At times we passed quite close to the mountains and it was when passing these that we kept our fingers crossed as it is in the mountains that the Ba Loo Jen and the bandits have their strongholds. We frequently met strong Japanese patrols patrolling the railway. Every station building in this area had been very thoroughly destroyed. Now and then a corpse or two would bear mute testimony of the struggle which was going on all the time.

We made a point of stopping every three hours in some village for a rest and some food. We found that the donkeys would eat anything from pear peelings and cores to a sort of wafer thin unleavened bread. The barrow men also ate the same unleavened bread and so did we and were glad to get it. The weather held and was not too hot, but of course it being dry the people in the rear were smothered in dust. Being the leader, I kept up a very fast pace as I realized that for safety's sake, we must get to Liang Hsiao Tien before dark. I got frequent S.O.S.s from the rear to slow down.

I went back and found many of the women in tears through sheer fatigue and one of the children, a sweet little girl of six, ill with a high temperature. I realized that the pace was far too hard for the mite, but as I have already said it was absolutely essential that we reach our destination before dark. So after dosing her with aspirin and multiple vitamin tablets, we strapped her onto the barrow and cracked on again. Finally at 7.00 p.m., a half an hour before dark, we reached Liang Hsiao Tlen. We had done it and were very happy about it, I can tell you. We managed to get into a caravanserai for the night, which was very fortunate as all the hostelries in towns and villages were generally packed with travellers who wished to avoid being out in the open country after dark.

Chen and I immediately set out to find out about trains and you can imagine our dismay when we learned that the Ba Loos had blown up the railway bridge just south of the town the night before. I am afraid that I was reduced to cursing loud and long! Further enquiries revealed that the nearest possible place for a train was a big town called Linchen, which was 32 miles further down the line and that meant another spell on Shanks' mare. But the motto had to be and was "Nil Desperandum." I broke the news to the rest of the members of the caravan and the expression on their faces were indescribable.

Before we had a bite to eat, we rounded up the leading barrow man and asked him what about it. His reply was a flat refusal. He was too tired! This was a poser, but friend Chen was equal to the occasion and after a solid hour of arguing, cajolery, threats and much hard swearing, the barrow man agreed to round up another gang of barrows and take us on. Chen, a Russian lad I called Mickey and I celebrated the victory at a street restaurant with a huge meal and did we need it! We spent a hectic hour rounding up the caravan and installing the men and animals in the compound. Little Ella, the sick girl, had made a remarkable recovery and was sleeping peacefully. We had managed to raise some hot water and gave her a good bath. Despite the braying of donkeys, the mosquitoes, the fleas, the bed bugs and my hard couch, I slept like a log and so did the rest of the party.

Up early next morning and we were on our way for what we hoped was the last walk. This time we had to march away from the railway line and cut across country as we had been warned that the Japs patrolling the line were very nervous and had got to the stage of shooting first and asking questions afterwards. This made us decide to risk falling in with Ba Loos and bandits by cutting across country through the hill passes and coming back on the line about four miles above Linchen. We passed through some truly lovely country. We called a halt every three and a half hours for a rest and food. The little girl stood up to the march very well and was most brave. We found the hinterland apparently untouched by the ravages of war and the people looking quite prosperous and well. They were all quite pleasant to us and full of curiosity, as we were the first white people they had seen for years.

About 1.00 p.m. we were stopped on the road by three rather tough looking individuals and asked who we were and where we were going. They were in civilian clothes, but all three carried ugly looking mauser pistols and whilst one of them did the questioning, the other two stood back and kept us covered. Chen very carefully explained that I was British and a returning P.O.W. and vaguely inferred that the rest of the foreigners were the same. I offered the leader a Chesterfield, which after some hesitancy, he accepted. Friendly relations being more or less established, I next offered him a drink of cognac which I had received from the German Fathers at Yenchowfu. I wished I hadn't because he liked it and emptied half the bottle without turning a hair. This last gesture, however, did the trick and they stepped aside and allowed us to carry on. They kept the caravan covered, however, until we had all passed and then walked across the fields to a village, set a short distance back from the road, and I heaved a big sigh of relief.

About 3.00 p.m. it started to rain. During the dry weather,

the roads are ankle deep in dust and you can imagine what it was like when it rained. We ploughed on through the mud and rain and reached the road running beside the railway at about 5.00 p.m. with still four or five miles to go. Our speed, due to the mud, had dropped to a snail's pace. Most of us had mud up to the waist and were wringing wet. It looked as if we wouldn't make Linchen until about 9 or 10 and none of us relished the prospect of entering a town full of very nervous soldiery after dark. However, the old saying, "Be it ever so dark, there is always a silver lining somewhere," proved to be correct, as far as we were concerned, for on looking back along the line we saw a train coming along. I sent Mickey, my aide-de-camp, across the fields to the line and told him to try and flag the train. Chen and I dashed back and chased up the stragglers.

By this time, the train — a military repair train — had rolled up and much to our joy pulled up. The Jap soldiers were very suspicious and kept us covered with machine guns and tommy guns. We were hardly recognisable as Europeans, as we were smothered in mud. We turned the barrows off the road and across the rain soaked fields, and what a job it was. Those poor donkeys certainly had sore hides that afternoon! Fortunately, the Jap officer understood a little English and after explaining who we were, he allowed us to board the train. Our accommodation was on top of rails and sleepers on a flat car. But did we care? Not a bit of it! We were headed for home and on a train even if it wasn't de luxe! We found out to our joy that a train would be leaving for Hsuchowfu next morning at about 9.30, but that the only accommodation available in Linchen was at the German Catholic Mission which was outside the town and would take at least three quarters of an hour to reach.

On arrival at Linchen, we commandeered the only two ricshas available in the town and also the station luggage carrier, piled all the luggage we could on these vehicles and ploughed through the mud to the other side of the town. We arrived at the city gate, which we found shut and heavily guarded by puppet troops. It was already dark and the guards refused to open up and let us out, saying that there were Ba Loos outside and that they might rush the gate. I pulled $400 out of my pocket and waved that under the nose of the sergeant. This overcame his scruples. He turned his guard out who manned their positions after which he opened the gate and let us through. If the road through the city was bad, the one outside was ten times worse. We were actually knee deep in mud and it was a tough job pushing the loaded ricshas and carrier through it. It took us a good three quarters of an hour to traverse the quarter mile to the mission gate.

The Fathers received us very kindly and made us welcome. This mission was a very poor one and they were living under constant threat of annihilation. Indeed, just a few days before they had been raided by Ba Loos who, after informing them that they had had orders to shoot all the Fathers and burn the mission down, had commenced operations by ransacking the place. However, in the middle of this, a Chinese civilian had walked into the courtyard and picked up one of the rifles piled there. One of the Ba Loos coming out of the Church seeing the man looking at the rifle pulled his pistol out and shot the man dead. The rest all rushed out and the Chief seeing the man's face, cried out that the dead man had been his best informer. After a considerable amount of confusion and shouting, they mournfully picked up the corpse and, taking their arms up, decamped, leaving the mission in peace. You can well imagine the feelings of the good Fathers at this almost miraculous deliverance from death.

The Fathers provided us with a frugal — but much appreciated — hot meal. They provided us also with sleeping accommodation and we were able to strip off and get our clothes dry. Shortly after ten that night, a terrific din broke out round the city. We could hear rifles, machine guns, trench mortars and field guns firing and also the bursting of hand grenades. Occasionally bullets whistled over the mission or flattened themselves against the wall. This went on till two in the morning. We learned next day that a strong force of Ba Loos had attacked the city, but that the attack had been beaten off by the Japs and their puppets.

We awoke at 5.30 to find it still raining. We packed up and loaded the ricshas which we had retained at the mission and after breakfast, we bid our kindly hosts goodbye and once more went out into the mud. We hadn't been able to see the road the night before, but now we could and what a road it was! The struggle through the mud was terrible. I fell a couple of times and you can imagine what I looked like. However, we finally managed to reach the station and, after considerable negotiation, we managed to get an open freight van allocated to us. What a fight to keep the mobs of Chinese off the van. We simply couldn't let them on as we should have been swamped and we had women and children with us. Using bamboo sticks, we kept them from climbing up the iron ladder on to the van. This went on until the train finally started. The journey, which should have only taken at the most four hours, took us nine. It pelted with rain, but did we care? Not us! We were headed, for Home!

About three hours journey from Hsuchowfu, we met the vanguard of the advancing Chinese troops coming to take over from the Japs. After the vanguard passed, we came on what appeared to be the main body. It was a remarkable sight. Thousands upon thousands of men and horses moving in masses across the countryside as far as the eye could see. At one station we were held up for four hours while troop train after troop train passed us. The Chinese on our train threw off all signs of fear and servility of and to the Japanese and loudly cheered the crowded troop trains. The Chinese soldiers cheered and waved back. We finally got moving again and arrived at Hsuchowfu at 7.30 p.m. It was still raining. We found our way to the Canadian Italian Mission, where we spent the night in warmth and comfort.

Next morning we went down to the station with the Bishop of Pengpu and his suite, he having very kindly invited us to share his carriage with him and spend the night at his mission in Pengpu which invitation, I need hardly say, we very gladly accepted. Arriving at Pengpu, we received a royal welcome, a good feed and a comfortable bed which was very much appreciated. The next morning, accompanied by some of the Fathers who were also going to Shanghai, we boarded the train and, after an uneventful trip, arrived at Pukow at about 5.00 p.m. We crossed the Yangtsze River by ferry and after a good meal at a Chinese restaurant, we arrived at Nanking Station. It was a struggle getting on the train, but we managed it all right. We travelled all that night and finally pulled into Shanghai, arriving at the same platform I had left just three months before as a prisoner. There is no need to describe my feelings. We disembarked and I got myself a pedicab and an hour later was enjoying a real hot bath at Home.

CHAPTER XVII
"LEST WE FORGET"

AFTER working for about a month in Shanghai, I was notified that I could proceed to Australia on leave. The trip and reunion with my family was much the same as that of thousands of others who had also been separated from their families. I was reluctant to return to this city where I had suffered so much mental and physical torment, but it was a case of "must do when the devil drives." Shortly after my return, I was summonsed by the British War Crimes Team to identify none other than Major, now Colonel, Nagata. How changed he was! No longer did his face carry the arrogant smile of the conqueror. He was down and he knew it.

He said that he did not know or remember anything about what had taken place in Bridge House during my incarceration therein, but on being pressed by his questioners, he finally said that if such things had taken place, then he, as the man in charge, must be held responsible. I could not help noting the difference in the manner in which he was questioned in comparison to the manner in which I was questioned, even though it was known that he was guilty, if not directly, at least indirectly, for the horrible things that had taken place in that dreadful institution known as Bridge House. There was no beating for him, no electrical torture, no water treatment, no being strung up by the thumbs, no starvation, indeed nothing of what we, his former victims, went through.

During the summer of 1947, I also appeared as a witness in

Odera (L) and Honda stand trial, 1947

the trials of Odera and Honda. There again, what a change in the demeanour of these two men, especially the arrogant swine Honda. He walked into the court room and gave us, his former charges, a sickly smile and a bow. He received nothing but stony looks in return. His feeble excuses during his trial were laughable. He got what was coming to him, but not nearly enough. Odera was sentenced to seven years imprisonment and Honda to ten years. One amusing incident during the trial was the showing of the pictures which I had taken at Fengtai and one small section which I had managed to take at Haiphong Road during the actual hostilities. While I was showing the pictures to the judges and the two defendants, I turned around and looked at Honda who was standing beside me, and the look of blank astonishment on his face when he saw the Haiphong Road pictures was amusing to see. You could see and feel the thought passing through his mind, "How in hell did this fellow get these pictures?"

On the 23rd September, 1948, I was again called as a witness at the trial of Nagata. He stood there in the dock, small and timid looking, every vestige of arrogance taken out of him. He had little or nothing to say, whilst the horrible story of Bridge House was recited to the judges. He was eventually sentenced to imprisonment for life.

Now what is the aim, the idea, behind the recital of this story? I do not advocate that every time a Briton or American meets a Japanese that he should slap him in the face, kick him or beat him. Certainly not. The Japanese have many good points and these points can be developed to the good of civilization, but the writer advocates that the occupation and/or surveillance of Japan should be kept up for not two, three, five or seven years, but for at least forty or fifty years. Those who are now in charge and hold the destiny of Japan in their hands, should not be hoodwinked by the apparent adoption of the principles of democracy by the Japanese people. That is a blind. The change is too sudden to be genuine. It must be remembered that the spirit of Bushido or Samuraism, feudalism and belief in the divinity of the Emperor, is bred right into the Japanese people.

This may be illustrated by the following incident. During the concert which the Japanese held in "celebration" of the opening of Haiphong Road camp on November 6th, 1944, item after item on the programme clearly illustrated this particular point. Children whose ages ranged from three to eight years of age came on to the stage, dressed in the ancient samurai costume and showed how glorious it was to die for their country, for their Emperor. The whole thing was a glorification of war! Their faces were stern, pitiless, with hatred looking out of their eyes, as they went through their act. They came on to the stage with a blood stained bandage on their heads. Facing the audience, they bowed low and then suddenly whipped out a sword. The act consisted of a sort of dance in which the actor represented a warrior surrounded by enemies. The actor hewed and cut his enemies down right and left. In return he received many blows, finally receiving the death blow. Finding himself overcome and in order to avoid capture, he sinks to his knees and raising his eyes to Heaven, reverses the sword and plunges the blade into his own bosom, sinking to the ground, dead.

That scene was enacted, as I have already said, over and over again, by children of three to eight years of age, both male and female. Their acts were frantically applauded by the audience, showing that they appreciated the scene that they had witnessed and agreed with the principle underlying the act. How can you hope to eradicate that spirit in the matter of two, three or four years? It is impossible, and the country must and should be kept properly supervised until those little children whom we saw acting in that play grow up and eventually die, and see that they do not pass on that spirit to the unborn millions of Japanese who are coming. Properly managed, properly organized, the Japanese can become a great and fine nation.

They should never again, however, be allowed in any way to become militarised. Allow them to have no navy, no army to speak of. Instead guarantee them protection from any outside aggression. Let them develop their country, their very beautiful country into a sort of Switzerland of the Orient. If you do not do this, the spirit of Bushido which is lying dormant will again rear its ugly head in the near future, and before you know it, they will be in a position to again strike. They are people that do not forget their mistakes, and, remembering those mistakes they made before, they will take care not to make them again and the next time the tables may be turned. Then, God help us all! I hope this story is read by those who have influence, who are in power and who will make sure that never again will the people of the world have to undergo the horror that they have gone through, that they did go through, during those years between December 8th, 1941, to August 15th, 1945.

Witnesses in the Bridge House War Crimes trial, photographed on their arrival from Shanghai by HMS Sussex. Left to right: Mr J.M. Watson, Mr J.R. Canning, Mr H. Pringle, Mr J. Eynstone, Mr D. Toeg, Dr Stephen Sturton and Mr R.C. Hillman (Source: Unknown newspaper)

AFTERWORD

By F. Eileen Gray (née Pringle), OAM

An edited transcript of "In Search of One's Identity," *an informal talk given to members of the Royal Asiatic Society China in Shanghai on August 29, 2008*

I AM not an historian and my talk tonight is not intended as a definitive history of John and Florence Pringle and their descendants in China. It will be predominantly personal recollections of my early years up to the age of thirteen in Shanghai to give you some idea of my life in this city then and the influence that it was to have over my future life in Australia. I will be setting those recollections within a framework of recent research into the Pringle family from 1890 to 1948.

A chance reply to my query earlier this year on the Old China Hands' web-site regarding information being sought on the old Shanghai British School began for me an amazing journey. First came Marigold Hogan who led me to Desmond Power, Eric Niderost, Greg Leck, Peter Hibbard, Gaythorne Sylvester, and finally Tess Johnston, all so willing to assist me to find out more about the old Shanghai, my life there before and after the War and the new and modern city which I was about to visit after a sixty year break. I had already met Anne Warr whose earlier advice and information had been so helpful in the search for my earlier life. Her book *Shanghai Architecture* has been of invaluable assistance and I have pored over it avidly.

I cannot recall just how many e-mails were exchanged once it was made known that I was the younger daughter of Henry

Forsythe Pringle who had written a book, yet to be published, about his dreadful experiences in World War II in Bridge House, a Japanese torture centre, and later in Haiphong Road Camp before finally ending up in Feng Tai Camp near Beijing. Greg Leck, in his remarkable book *Captives of Empire: The Japanese Internment of Allied Civilians in China 1941-1945*, has quoted from my father's book. I have since been in touch with Greg and he now has a copy of the film footage Dad took of some of his internment.

But I am leaping ahead too fast and I need to take you back to England where this whole saga truly began.

Growing up in a busy household, it never seemed the right time to sit down and talk about one's ancestors and the little I gleaned had to suffice. However, as a result of becoming ill at the end of 2007, I finally found the time to start that inevitable research program which is essential in discovering facts about family. My husband's research skills and patience were inevitably the basis of my success for which I thank him most sincerely. My parents had both gone many years before I was bitten by the family history bug so I had to rely on what little memories I had, supplemented by research of some primary and secondary sources.

Sadly, I never met my paternal grandparents or my wonderful Uncle Jack who were long gone by the time I arrived on the scene. My grandfather, John Pringle was born in New Hartley, Northumberland in 1863 into a coal mining family. My grandmother, Florence Eugene Pringle (née Marsh) was born in Lambeth, Surrey c.1858 and was listed as a seamstress in the census of 1881. Both came from large families with brothers and sisters who were never mentioned to me by my father. It was not until I began my research that I discovered suddenly I was part of a large family. It is also interesting to note that my maternal great grandfather was listed as an artist, and sometimes I wonder whether my love of needlework, art, and music all originate from my grandmother's gene pool. Are they all coincidences? Somehow it makes me feel closer to these grandparents and uncle I never knew.

In the mid-1800s, the British Empire was at its zenith and the colonies were places to where those seeking to extend their horizons were encouraged to go. With Britain's natural resources and land area dwindling and the call of the colonies motivating the young folk to take opportunities, it is not surprising that John Pringle, a young coal miner, perhaps struggling to survive the problems at home, sought further adventures elsewhere. The rest is history.

With shipping lists before 1890 difficult to find, I cannot say just when they both left England, but by the time the census of 1891 was taken, both John and Florence had left to seek their fame and fortune, as they say, in China. In 1870, the Chinese were able to only mine small outcrops of coal, and were seeking new forms of mining. They must have welcomed the advent of the experienced British with their more modern machinery. New deeper coal seams were discovered and exploited in many areas in this vast country, but Grandfather chose the northern areas around Tientsin (Tianjin).

Why my grandmother went there intrigues me, but I can only surmise she journeyed there as a companion/seamstress to a wife of a British professional, also in the coal mining industry. The next stage of their life is therefore only my imaginings for I have not as yet made any further inroads into their early life in this new and totally different country. Like most people in a foreign land, I think, they would have tended to mingle in their own social circles.

The marriage of John Pringle and Florence Eugene Marsh was registered as celebrated at the British Consulate in Tientsin on 2 April 1892, his professional status being a coal-mining engineer while she had none. Her father, Watson Fullerton Marsh, recorded as an artist, and his father, Joseph Pringle, a coal-mining engineer, are the only other people mentioned on the certificate. My Uncle Jack, christened as John Dunbar Marsh, was born in Tongshan on 1 September 1893, with my grandfather still listed as a coal mining engineer. From that time, I have absolutely no knowledge of their lives in that area of China. But I have read stories of other British folk in China that have given me some insight into the life style of these early settlers.

Nine years after the birth of my uncle, my father Henry Forsythe was born, in Tongshan on 2 December 1902, two years after the Boxer Rebellion.

Many years later, while sitting with my ailing father in the Intensive Care Unit of our hospital in Canberra, he began to tell me a little more of his life as a young boy. Names like 'Pingtao', 'Chinwangtao', and 'Shanhaikwan' were mentioned. He told me how as a boy he had played in the shadow of the Great Wall of China, that his mother later ran a guest house which I presume was for British residents and that he, my father, only spoke Chinese until the age of five. The latter I can easily believe, for he spoke Chinese fluently all his life. I gather both parents were so busy with their lives and so, with their children only mixing with the servants' children, this was inevitable.

My father told me of an incident when his father spoke to him and he replied in Chinese. My grandfather then asked him to please speak in English. With the discovery that his sons were unable to speak the mother tongue, Grandfather and Florence made the decision to move to Shanghai, where my father was put into the American School in around 1907.

My grandfather later worked in Shanghai, and I quote from my uncle's obituary: "The deceased's parents, who died only recently, were well known both in Tientsin and Shanghai and prior to his death his father was employed in the Public Works Department of the Municipal Council, latterly at Kangchiao Quarries." (*North China Herald*, 17 March 1923, page 729). It is believed he became an Inspector of Public Works. My father once remarked that my grandfather helped build the roads in Shanghai—to what extent that is true, I cannot say.

He also seemed to be involved with surveying, perhaps in relation to coal deposits. I have in my possession a hand written passport type document in Chinese in which it states that

'Mr Pringle, a trainee engineer' was given permission to travel through various areas of China to assist in surveying and mapping new areas. This document is very old and was issued on the authority of Emperor Kwang-Su who died in 1909. It was authorised on 19 November in the 20th year of the Emperor's reign. Thus we know the passport was for my grandfather, John Pringle.

In 1909, my Uncle Jack left to work on rubber plantations in Malaya until 1912. My father would have been just 7 years old at the time and must have missed his brother enormously as they were very close. Both were musicians — my uncle played several instruments while my father had a deep and rich bass voice. That love of music my father passed on to me.

After these years away, Jack moved back to China — he would have been 19 years old. Where he moved after this time, I cannot say but I believe it was to England, where he worked prior to serving in World War I, during which time he rose to the rank of Captain.

Florence, my grandmother, in the meantime had not been well for some time with a weak chest and, as reported in the *North China Herald* on 8 September 1917, died on 3 September 1917. Her address was given as 13 Kungping Rd (now Gongping Lu) Shanghai and her age as 54. She was buried at Bubbling Well Cemetery (now Jing'an Park). It has intrigued my husband and I as to her reported age, for by our reckoning she would have been 59, though Dad always told me she was 57. Was the year of her birth mistakenly recorded on her birth certificate?

I would like to add at this point that the discovery of my grandmother's death notice filled me with very deep emotion. For the first time in my life since my own parents had gone, I felt I had a paternal family whom I knew so little about. More research uncovered many great aunts and uncles as well.

My father at the time of his mother's death would have been 15 and a very carefree young man. He told me many tales of boyhood revelry and a developing great love of Shanghai and its surrounding countryside. There he rode, played, hunted and grew into a young man with a great zest for life. First mention of the Shanghai Volunteer Corps enters his life, an interest in which his brother was also involved later after his return from World War I.

In the *North China Herald* on 11 January 1919, page 120, the death of my grandfather was reported as at age 55. He also was buried at Bubbling Well Cemetery. This threw Henry out of his comfort zone completely for he was now an orphan with his brother far away in England. During the latter part of the year following his father's death Henry, now aged almost 17, sailed to England to join his brother who was by then running a small business in London after the war. He worked as a motor mechanic for twopence an hour.

Shortly after, he joined the army, easily putting up his age to 17 as he was so tall. Having been in the Shanghai Volunteer Corps since he was 15, he must have been very strong for his age. He joined the Grenadier Guards Machine Gun Regiment in Chatham in early December 1919 and stood guard outside Buckingham Palace, where he was reputed to have held a short conversation with King George V. He was transferred to another Battalion of the Grenadier Guards before returning by ship to Shanghai, departing 5 November, 1922 and arriving back home on 22 December. The lack of mention of his name in the incoming shipping news in the *North China Herald* confirms he travelled as crew. I learned later that he had worked his passage across to China as a cabin steward.

His brother Jack had married Violet Strachan in London sometime between July and September, 1919. They had a son John F. H. Pringle some time between October and December 1920. Jack and his family sailed for Shanghai aboard the P&O Ship *Kashmir* on 7 June 1922.

On my father's return to China 6 months later he possibly lived with his brother and his family. I have no definite information other than to say he worked with Customs for some time and with British American Tobacco. He told me many tales of his expeditions up the river on his many missions in search of smugglers. It was during this time that he learned the true tragedy of Rabies when a fellow officer's daughter suffered the dreaded disease after being bitten by a rabid dog.

Within a few months of his return to Shanghai, Henry's brother died suddenly on 12 March 1923. He succumbed to the mustard gas poisoning he had suffered in World War I and, as a result of an emergency appendectomy, he died of pneumonia at the Victoria Nursing Home in Shanghai at the age of 29. He also was buried at Bubbling Well Cemetery.

Having read his obituary in the *North China Herald*, 17 March 1923 it was obviously a very impressive service, for, "Captain John Pringle was taken by gun carriage through Shanghai flanked by his fellow officers from the Shanghai Volunteer Corps. Deepest sympathies were extended to his widow and child in their sudden bereavement. The chief mourners were his widow and brother. The 'Last Post' having been played, the firing party fired a volley. Many beautiful floral offerings were sent."

I have no further information on the whereabouts of Violet and little John after this, although I believe they eventually returned to England.

While in England, my father Henry had met Isabel Peake, to whom he became engaged. They were both very young and the long separation with her still in England and he back in China did nothing to cement the relationship. However, she eventually travelled to Shanghai to marry him and their wedding was written up in detail in the *North China Herald* on 12 December 1925, page 482. The minister was The Very Reverend C.J.F. Symons. The names mentioned in the report include, Mr and Mrs W. R. Knox, Miss Lilian Curtiss, Miss Dorothy Knox, Mr J. V. Webb and Mr H. Dayton.

Unfortunately, youth and inexperience caused irreparable harm and 12 months later the marriage was annulled. Henry was alone again. However they remained firm friends for the rest of their lives. Her subsequent married name was Isabel Duck.

My mother, Isabella Holmes, born on 2 November 1894, a Scottish Queen's Nurse, also from a large family of seven children, had arrived in Shanghai by ship on an unknown date in the mid 1920s to further her studies in infectious diseases. She was given a position at the Shanghai Municipal Council Sanatorium in Hungjao (Hongqiao) Road. I have a letter in my possession written by the patients on 25 November 1929 to my mother when she left for another appointment elsewhere. It contains their deepest thanks from them all for her expert care and her 'mothering' of them. From the signatures they appeared to be Russians, Japanese, British, and Italian. I vaguely remember her telling me that for a period of time she worked in the Isolation Hospital, but have no further information.

She soon became a member of the social set and it was there she met my father Henry — they became engaged in 1928. I have a few photos of their engagement time spent with friends riding, boating, partying, all fitting into what I would have imagined was a busy professional time at the Isolation Hospital for my mother. How happy they all were, enjoying the delights that Shanghai offered. They did not marry till 15 April, 1932 at the Holy Trinity Cathedral in Shanghai. Their bridesmaid was Eva Hordern and Len Fisher was the best man — the latter became my godfather. By this time, my father had been working for the Shanghai Telephone Company, Nanjing Rd for a few years and was still a member of the Shanghai Volunteer Corps as a 2nd Lieutenant.

In 1935 Isabella and Henry adopted a White Russian baby Lubove Vasiievna born on 23 September to Vasili Andreevitch Gladisheff and Claudia Fedorovna Gladisheff in Shanghai. With two small children already, the baby's family were so impoverished, the father had to kill dogs to feed his family, so I was told. The baby had been fed with flour and water instead of milk taken by the amah for her own children, and developed rickets and ulcers on her tiny body. The chance that her baby would be taken great care of by a medically well-educated Nursing Sister gave Lubove's mother the courage to give her child up for adoption. The tiny baby was re-named Elizabeth Doreen and baptised in the Holy Trinity Church on 12 May 1935. Her godfather was Max Speigler. With careful nursing by my mother her health improved and by the time I arrived on 19 March 1936 at Paulun Hospital (now Changzheng Hospital) she was a beautiful little 18 month old child. I should mention here that my sister has written memoirs of her life to 2005, entitled *In Search of Lubove**, which includes recollections of her time in Shanghai.

Life was good for the Pringles, but in 1937 as a result of the 'Battle for Shanghai', Mother took her two babies to Hong Kong, returning when hostilities had ceased. My father remained in Shanghai as a member of the Shanghai Volunteer Corps. Prior to this time, my sister and I had an amah named Trilby whose precious, long-awaited son my mother saved when very ill – my mother was shown such devotion by amah for the rest of her time with us. We then had a Portuguese nanny named Julie.

During the period of their early parenthood, they lived at a number of addresses. Thanks to the research of Peter Hibbard, we know these to have included: from 1935 to 1937 at Georgia Apartments numbers 61 and 72, Ave Petain (now 331 Hengshan Lu); in 1939 at 302 Route Charles Culty (now Hunan Lu) and finally from 1940 at House 34, Lane 910 Yuyuen Rd. Chingle Lu also rings a bell, but I have no research to support it.

Both my parents had other interests beyond the social scene and their children. My father was very heavily involved in the Masons, an interest he had shared with his brother before his death. My father rose to very high ranks in several Lodges over his 60-year membership both in Shanghai and Australia, while my mother, ever the student, had begun her life-long interest and study in Comparative Religions. Dad was also very energetic with his activities with the Shanghai Volunteer Corps. Medals now held by our son Michael, recorded that Henry earned recognition as a 2nd Lieutenant during the years

1917-1918, 1923-1927 and 1934-1940. He was also awarded another medal by the Shanghai Municipal Council for services rendered in the Battle for Shanghai from 12 August-26 November 1937 by which time it is believed he had attained the level of Major.

Life continued to be a round of dinner parties with friends of all nationalities. Children were given lavish birthday parties, usually in fancy costume. At one Christmas party my sister was dressed as one of Santa's elves and I as a fairy in a lemon satin dress with wings, and we even had the Xmas Angel appear! Another time Elizabeth wore a soft apricot coloured sari and I attended as a little Dutch girl, clogs and all. My mother, always ready for some fun, dressed in a gipsy outfit and my father in his Shanghai Volunteer Corps uniform. Life was so deliciously happy and enriched with ballet classes at Audrey King's studio and concerts at the Lyceum Theatre, where all the students were involved with more beautiful costumes made by our tailor.

In 1938, we went on home leave to Scotland, where we met up with my mother's relatives, several aunts and uncles, on the Isle of Arran. Pictures of us all enjoying the wonderful activities on the farm with the goats and Dad driving a tractor still give me much pleasure. Sadly, that was to be the last contact with my mother's family. My return there in 1999, while on a tour of Scotland, was very nostalgic.

Back home, the political scene was changing as war in Europe soon spread to the East and, by 1941, it was obvious the situation was worsening.

My sister had started school the year before at the Cathedral Girls School in Ave Haig (now Huashan Lu) that was to become the Shanghai British School after the war. In March 1941, I too started at the school and was settled and happy though I don't recall those times at all, except for my uniform which was blue with a white collar and long white socks and a straw hat.

All I can recall of my first 5 1/2 years was climbing the water tower on top of an apartment house, probably the Picardie, at the age of 2 1/2; having fairy birds flying round the closed-in verandah of our apartment when I was about 3 1/2; and chooks in the back garden in Yuyuen Road. There were also our dolls' houses and dolls, ballet concerts and the many parties.

This was all to change dramatically in October 1941 when my father sent my mother and his two girls to Australia aboard the SS *Nellore*. The Japanese later sank it.

Dad stayed behind as many of the fathers did to settle their affairs and watch our home. He was arrested by the Japanese Kempetei for alleged subversive activities and, though innocent, was thrown into Bridge House on 6 October 1942. Here he suffered terribly at his captors' hands. His story can be read in detail in this book. Greg Leck's book previously referred to tells much of the story of imprisonment of civilians which can still bring tears to the eyes of readers after all this time. Deprivation, starvation and incarceration are only some of the horrors they endured. Yet the spirit of survival is strong in humans and many lived to tell the tale and record their stories for posterity.

For us in Australia, as refugees, we faced different challenges but our determined Scottish mother faced these adversities with her usual strength of character, which is a great story for another time. Needless to say, we moved from area to area, as the mistrusting Australians who were sending thousands of their own boys to the front to be massacred by the opposing forces did not readily accept refugees. Eventually after a period of time, ten different Primary schools and many less than acceptable rental accommodation places, we ended up in a lovely area of Sydney and lived out our war years in thankful freedom. Mother's hoarding of the precious jars of peanut butter is still vivid in our minds. On my father's final return to us, she proudly brought them out for him, at the sight of which he was almost ill, as he recalled the endless jars of it mixed with flour that was at times their only food.

At the end of the war, the Red Cross directed my father to return to us in Australia. At the time, after his experiences in prison and his long trek back to Shanghai from Peking after his release, he was exhausted emotionally, mentally and physically. For these reasons he was loath to return to the family he had not seen since 1941. The trek back to Shanghai is recorded in his book and is an amazing journey of determination and hardship for one who had suffered so badly for years.

The terrible day when this stranger knocked on our front door in Sydney and asked to see Mother is burnt into my memory for at first we did not recognise him. The gaunt-faced, haggard man was not the hale and hearty man we had left behind. With careful nursing and much welcoming on behalf of church friends and neighbours, he began to return to better health as we spent many months showing him the beauties of Australia and our happy, though simple, life style.

My father was determined, however, to return to Shanghai and pick up the threads of our old lives. On 10 January 1947, Mother and we two girls sailed for Shanghai aboard the SS *Taiping* and the Dutch ship the *Tjisdane* from Hong Kong. Dad had returned to Shanghai earlier, to prepare the way for us, aboard the RAN naval ship the HMAS *Alacrity*.

We happily moved into House 7 Lane 207 Wuyi Road and thus began for Elizabeth and I, our second sojourn in Shanghai. We were enrolled in the Shanghai British school and enjoyed the new challenges and life there after the devastating war years.

Having brought bikes with us from Australia my sister and I rode to school every day, starting school at 8.10 am and finishing at 1.10 pm. On Saturday mornings we rode to our piano lessons with a Professor Zak in Ave Joffre (now Huaihai Lu). I can still recall cold winter days when we bought hot chestnuts from a vendor cooking them in a huge old oil barrel filled with hot coals. We delighted in the flooding of the Huangpu River when we were driven to school in Dad's company car.

My sister and I enjoyed such a free life style as we rode wherever we wanted. Happily we went to a swimming pool on a wealthy Chinese family's estate and, on the weekends, out to

Hungjao (Hongqiao) past villagers washing their clothes in the creeks, or their rice for dinner and rode on narrow paths separating the paddy fields. Our first encounter with a funeral pyre piled high with coffins awaiting a mass cremation fascinated us, but the little bundles left on the roadside each late afternoon for the night cart to pick up saddened us greatly as we were told they were dead babies.

As the riding school was close by, we attended riding lessons each Friday evening which we both enjoyed. I can recall buying an Eskimo Toffee on our way home, for 500 dollars — that was really about a halfpenny in our currency back in Australia. Inflation was rife and Dad brought his pay home each week in a suitcase.

I often rode alone out into the further eastern areas of the French Concession to find newsagents to buy my beloved paper dolls. Back at home, I would go with my precious cargo and spend hours happily on my own cutting them out, dressing them and making up stories about all the characters. This remained a passion for me into my early teens but like all youthful pastimes, they eventually leave you. However they formed the basis for my great love of theatre throughout my life with all its beautiful costumes and make-believe stories.

I had several school friends though my best friend was Josephine Henry who lived with her family in an apartment closer into the city than I. Many weekends were spent at her place as we attended cinemas. I was sad to say good-bye to her when it was time to leave, she for Canada and us back to Australia.

My sister, being 18 months older than I, found teenage friendships more to her liking. She spent many hours with international friends from school doing what teenage girls loved doing even then, talking about clothes, fashions and boys.

School was not always happy, as we had many teachers who had suffered from incarceration and held many hidden agendas. People were struggling to come to terms with the loss of family members and homes and it was taking a long time to recover from such losses. But we children seemed to be sheltered from most of that, except that my father's war-related rages, brought on by the simplest occurrences, often had my sister and I in fear in our bedroom.

Dad's serious illness was to follow in 1948 after the War Crime Trials in Hong Kong, where the perpetrators of the atrocities were finally imprisoned for many years. The aftermath of the war years resulted in Dad's almost fatal attack of pneumonia and he was hospitalised for several weeks. Once again our mother protected us from the worst and we survived the episode with few scars. A ten-week vacation in Taiwan followed.

Back in Shanghai, after Taiwan, we resettled into our life and school resumed. Together with our friends from UNRAA and CNRRA we made our own films with villains and a nurse to assist the hero and even a Fairy Godmother. Sadly we were not given copies of these films as the Producer took them all with him when he left China. There were fetes and British traditional happenings at school, including the crowning of the May Queen and sports' days. There was Girl Guides, which included riding around Shanghai on buses to venues where badges were examined — one place I recalled going to was the YMCA building across the road from today's People's Park for my Swimmer's Badge.

There were visits to the Shanghai Rowing Club to swim, the Country Club, the Columbia Country Club and to Siccawei Convent (now Xujiahui Cathedral). At the latter, Mother bought magnificently embroidered cushion covers and a beautifully embroidered family table cloth with all our initials on it and the wide lace edging also carried out by the Chinese Nuns. Such beautiful work — and I still have the latter.

Dad proudly showed us where he used to race when young at the Shanghai Racecourse (now People's Square), and told us how he was Shanghai Tennis Champion back in the 1930s and Champion Cross Country Runner.

For me personally, the most exciting time in those two years after the war were the wonderful concerts we attended where

The author's wife, Isabella (1946), and family (1947)

friends of ours were the guest artists. I remember one charming and talented pianiste Leyda Ungerer, who played Tchaikowsky's No. 1 Concerto with the Shanghai Symphony Orchestra, conducted by Professor Foa. I recall also our delightful Irish friend Molly Burke, who worked for either CNRRA or UNRRA, with her magnificent contralto voice, singing from Gluck's "Orpheus and Eurydice". I still thrill to the music of these works and recall those happy days. I can even remember the beautiful golden dress Aunty Leyda wore that afternoon and the wonderful party we all attended afterward at Professor Foa's apartment. Leyda sadly died of cancer a few years later after returning to live with her husband and son in Germany, and Molly, too, in England a few years ago.

I can recall Mother teaching Boy that he must always boil the drinking water and each morning she would religiously go down to the kitchen to make sure he carried out the task before storing it in the empty Gilbey's Gin Bottles in the fridge. I can never see one of those bottles that I don't remember that fridge with the bottles lined up — 'dead marines' — from all the cocktails Dad made each evening for cocktail hour. I recall the delicious Black Forest Cake Leyda always brought to our parties and how we all sat round and played Bingo and later round the piano to hear Leyda play. Dad's great love was the black eggs that were always evident on the dining table at those parties.

American food parcels were still being handed around the freed internees and how my sister and I enjoyed the exotic foodstuffs inside those wonderful packages. Solid chocolate blocks which reminds me of the tale Dad told about when many of the prisoners received their parcels and, having gobbled down the chocolate, would bring it all back up because their poor systems were unable to digest such richness. Even we relished those parcels for food was scarce in Australia too and rations prevailed for a long time, as in Britain.

We had pets too, many ducks, hens, cats and one little Scotty Terrier, Julie. As we lived next door to a soap factory with a woven bamboo fence in Wuyi Lu, the ducks, cats and hens all ended up on someone's dinner table, I would think, for they mysteriously disappeared in rapid succession. As for Julie she was eventually given to a friend of Dad's who was prepared to take care of her after we left.

I remember a plane tree in our back garden that inevitably keeled over each time the city was flooded by the rising Huangpu River. Out would go Dad in his gumboots to prop it up yet again. I looked for it a few days ago while visiting Wuyi Road and alas it has not survived.

One memory of our first days back in Shanghai in 1947 was my flight from the balcony outside our parents' bedroom, to the hard ground below. Too influenced by an older sister who dared me to jump, I took off into space. I was lucky I was not killed, but the Gods smiled on me that day and being so young and very lightweight I think my guardian angels must have assisted my flight allowing me to suffer only some pain on landing to teach me a lesson. My sins were soon discovered when, walking to school to enrol shortly after the fateful day, my mother caught me limping and I was rushed by pedicab to the nearest Doctor's surgery. Harking back to before the war I remember swallowing a pin when just a toddler. I was told I had to eat mashed potato by the bowlful and having to be x-rayed in a huge machine, the location of which I cannot remember but in one of Shanghai's large hospitals or Doctor's rooms.

Another time I was bitten by a dog in a Chinese farmer's garden when just 5 years old. My parents, who were enjoying time in Jessfield Park (now Zhongshan Park), — the farm being next door — were there to rescue me and I recall being rushed to the Lister Institute to have the wound cauterised and 12 large injections in my abdomen over several weeks to stave off the dreaded rabies. The fact that as young children we should not have been trespassing was never mentioned again. My many spills off my bike in future years pale into insignificance after that particular adventure. I was always an accident waiting to happen!

Those were halcyon days for us all but the threat from the north was moving closer. My sister and I were sometimes attacked on our way to school and spat on and told to 'get out you dirty foreigners'.

The net was closing in, and fearful of being taken prisoner again my father could not get out of Shanghai fast enough. It was 1948, and once again we were bound for Australia. Once again our few possessions were packed and sent ahead of us by ship while Mother boxed up our few priceless Chinese treasures, household goods and clothes into trunks and cases yet again.

How that must have broken their hearts for, despite establishing new foundations and such plans for us as a family living abroad, their dreams were stripped away, leaving us vulnerable in the face of further adversity. My 46-year-old father's heartbreak at leaving his beloved China and the life we led there, not wealthy but so culturally rich, has stayed with me all my life. Frustrating though it is now, thinking we were back in China for good, we did not travel further than Taiwan during those two years, though my father returned to Beijing after the war.

Out to Lungwha airport we travelled, only to discover the plane was not ready for departure, so home we came to an almost empty house. I remember little of that day except that Dad took us out to dinner and a movie.

The day finally dawned and our departure was imminent. We boarded our aircraft, a small DC3, VR-HDJ, along with about 20 other passengers — several Chinese, mostly British, and several recorded as stateless. The flight was via Hong Kong, Manila, Darwin, Mt Isa and eventually Sydney. It was a most terrifying flight and my father said his heart broke as we tumbled about in the turbulence for some time, luggage flying around the cabin, the airhostess, Mary Wheeling, knocked out and dragged up to the cockpit. When he saw the look of absolute terror on my face he asked himself — what had he done to his children and his wife and why had he put us through that dreadful ordeal? But one has only to read his book of war experiences to know exactly why he did it. I never blamed him for that journey, for I have heard so many stories of those who suffered terribly because they stayed in China.

It is fascinating in a way to look back on those many thousands of people in Shanghai alone who struggled to gain a foothold back into Shanghai after the ravages of five years of war. To see their hopes and dreams of taking hold of their once happy and challenging lives snatched away from them yet again must have been so hard.

For my beloved parents it was a very difficult time, having to establish from the beginning their third home, as they had to re-adjust back into the then simpler Australian way of life. The stimulating social scene, the diverse Chinese culture, the exciting way of life, all had to be changed. My father was often out of work and how my mother managed to raise us two girls on the pittance he eventually earned amazed me. We met many new people in similar circumstances to us, both Australian and international, who enriched my sister's and my life with their determination and belief in a better world, for which I am eternally grateful.

This story is only one of thousands, and I thank you for giving me the opportunity to share it with you. At this point I would like to acknowledge China and its people, for they too had their desperate problems for many, many years after we departed.

F. Eileen Gray (née Pringle), OAM
August 29, 2008

Contact for further information:
Mrs F. Eileen Gray, 9/146 Shackleton Circuit, Mawson, ACT, 2607, Australia

* Enquiries as to the availability of Elizabeth's memoirs can be addressed to: Elizabeth Watson, 61 Bent Street, Cooma, NSW, 2630, Australia.

Other Books
in the Earnshaw Books
China Classics
Series

See
www.TalesOfOldChina.com/store
for details